THREE
TIMES Up

BY WINSON ELGERSMA
B.A., B.D., LL.B.

 **FriesenPress**

Suite 300 – 852 Fort Street
Victoria, BC, Canada V8W 1H8
www.friesenpress.com

Copyright © 2014 by Winson Elgersma
First Edition — 2014

ISBN
978-1-4602-4690-0 (Hardcover)
978-1-4602-4691-7 (Paperback)
978-1-4602-4692-4 (eBook)

1. Biography & Autobiography, Personal Memoirs

Distributed to the trade by The Ingram Book Company

THREE
TIMES Up

— *a memoir* —

TABLE OF CONTENTS

TIMELINE

Date	Event
September 4, 1943	My birthday
April 16, 1944	Joyce's birthday
September 1963	I moved to Sioux Center, Iowa and enrolled at Dordt College
August 10, 1966	Joyce and I are married
August 1967	Moved to Grand Rapids, Michigan, and enrolled at Calvin Theological Seminary
February 14, 1968	Delbert is born
August 15, 1969	Vincent is born

August 1970	Moved back to Iowa and I began my first career as a minister in the Christian Reformed Church
February 2, 1973	Laura is born
October 1973	I left the ministry and we moved to Edmonton, Alberta
February 1974	I began my second career as a real estate agent
May 31, 1976	Chadwin is born
September 1976	I was promoted to manager of a real estate office
September 1977	We moved into our new home in Westridge
August 1978	Accidently "met" Queen Elizabeth

September 1982	Enrolled at the University of Alberta Law School
April 1986	Graduated from Law School and began my articles with the Federal Department of Justice
August 1987	I was admitted to the bar and I began my third career as a lawyer, in Red Deer, Alberta
September 1988	Joyce, Laura and Chad joined me in Red Deer
November 1997	We moved to Sylvan Lake and into our new home that Joyce designed
November 2004	I retired and we moved to Vancouver Island

INTRODUCTION

This is the story of my life. For years people have urged me to record it. I resisted, not because of the effort required, but because of the time. Now, I am retired. I also have my own reasons for wanting to chronicle my life. Joyce and I lived through three careers. The nature of the work was such that children were seldom present. Hence, the three careers we lived were largely unknown to them. Hopefully, these memoirs will shed some light on the path of life on which we walked and occasionally fell.

All of our children are now grown and have families of their own. They are all busy. They all understand how daily needs attempt to elbow out the time their children also want. The same was true for us. I am now so very grateful that throughout our three careers we had one priority; the children came first. To that end, we agreed that until the children started school, Joyce would be home for them.

Under difficult circumstances she managed. If there were a Mother's Lifetime Achievement award, Joyce would be a contender. What follows is also her story.

All of our children were excellent students. I believe it was because of the time that Joyce spent with them when they were young. For Joyce, being a mother meant not just providing for their physical needs, but providing everything she could to shape and stimulate their minds.

On one occasion Joyce had taken all the children to her parents in Montana. She had decided to go by air. Chad was an infant, Laura was a toddler and the two older boys were active. While at the airport, in her own quiet and gentle way, Joyce was trying to keep control of all the children. A lady had been watching her for some time. Finally she said, "I've been watching you. You will get your reward in heaven."

That of course may be true. But I believe that Joyce has already seen her reward. All of our children are wonderful and caring people. They are all successful.

Delbert (Del) graduated from high school in 1985. He then went to Calvin College in Grand Rapids, Michigan for 1½ years. He loved Calvin and was a member of their swim team. They competed against various colleges and universities. Unfortunately, he could not afford to continue. In January 1987 he transferred to the University of Alberta (U of A). In 1988, after only 1½ years at the U of A, he was admitted to the University of British Columbia (U.B.C.) Law School. He was the youngest student in B.C. to be admitted to the bar. He is now practicing law on Vancouver Island. His firm, called "Beacon Law," has three offices.

Vincent (Vince) graduated from high school in 1987. He went to the U of A for one year, to Calvin College for one year, and back to the U of A for another year. After only three years he was admitted to the U of A Medical School. He graduated from med school with honors. He was fifth in a class of 120 students. In his graduation ceremony he received several awards. He is now a medical doctor in Brooks, Alberta. He is also a clinical lecturer in the Department of Family Medicine at the University of Calgary.

Laura graduated from high school in 1990. Thereafter she attended Red Deer College. She then transferred to the University of Calgary where she obtained her degree in Education. After her graduation she taught at Calgary Christian School for five years. She won the "Best Teacher of the Year" award in the very first year it was introduced. She is now farming with her family on Vancouver Island.

Chadwin (Chad) graduated from high school in 1994. Thereafter he attended Trinity Western University for two years and Red Deer College for one and a half. He then worked in the Alberta oil patch until the fall of 1998, at which time he was accepted by the Palmer Chiropractic School in Davenport, Iowa. He graduated in 2002 and for two years worked as a chiropractor. After that he enrolled in a medical school in Erie, Pennsylvania, from which he graduated in 2008. He is currently working as a board certified anesthesiologist in Buffalo, New York.

These memoirs are dedicated to our children and grandchildren, with love.

My story is from memory only. As such it is subject to the normal deficiencies of memory. I have not fact-checked every detail, date or dialogue. There may be some errors, but the gist of the story is true.

I have changed some names and omitted others. This is to protect the identity of those who did no wrong. The subject matter of each conversation is factual. However, the dialogue is recreated.

Our Family (from back to front)
Vincent, Delbert, Chadwin, Laura, Winson, Joyce

CHAPTER 1

LIFE AT HOME

My life began on September 4, 1943. I was raised on a farm near Neerlandia, Alberta, a Dutch farming community about ninety miles northwest of Edmonton. I was the third child of eight.

By far the greatest influence in my early life was my father. He was a wonderful man and I loved and admired him. My earliest memories of him are of a fun-loving person who was clearly happy with the circumstances of his life. He adored his wife, and she adored him. He enjoyed his children (at least most of the time). He loved farming. He was happy and thankful. Often while he was working we would hear him sing. He had a remarkably good voice. He was also an excellent yodeler. We loved to hear him yodel – not only because he did it well – but

1

when he yodeled we knew he was happy with us.

Saturday evenings were family nights. We had no television. Mom would always make something special and Dad would usually tell stories. Through these stories he would transport us into the adventurous and mischievous world he had known as a boy.

My parents were Christians and they raised us accordingly. Before every meal my father would pray. After every meal he would read a chapter from the Bible and pray. Each child also prayed. Sundays were for worship. There were two services at the local church, one in the morning and one in the afternoon. On Sunday evenings the teenagers went to Young People's Society which was basically a Bible study.

The most important and ultimate goal of my Christian parents was to see their children become Christian; that is, to see them accept Jesus as their Lord and Saviour. The day we publicly professed our faith, in church, was a day of celebration. My parents often prayed for their children's spiritual wellbeing.

Notwithstanding their faith, my parents were not prudes. They believed that salvation was a gift for which they were thankful. One cannot be thankful and spiteful or bitter at the same time. They loved life and had fun.

One Saturday evening Dad decided to teach us to dance. At least that's what he called it. In turn, he took each of his children and put their little feet on his big feet. Then in rhythm to the music on the radio he would side step from the kitchen to the hallway and back. During my turn, my nose began to bleed. I do not know why. I was not hurt but I cried anyway. As a third child you seized whatever attention you could get.

**My Mom and Dad as they were
when when I was a boy**

* * * * *

The family farm as it was when I was a boy.

For a child, life in a large family on the farm was nearly perfect. Unfortunately, we had no way of knowing how perfect it was. We had nothing to compare it to. As a result, we were not nearly as grateful as we should have been.

Farming is one of those few occupations where children can work along side their parents. In doing so, I believe that children gain an appreciation for what their parents do. Time is shared and it gives parents unexpected opportunities to pass on their values. Farming also has its downside. Children can be exposed to unforeseen risk and danger. They cannot always be supervised.

For reasons none of us can remember, Sandra (my older sister), and Andrew (my older brother) and I began to sniff gasoline. It was summer and in hot weather gas evaporates easily. The fumes were intoxicating and we were addicted. The effect was mind altering. Initially the mind provided a color show, which transformed into fireworks. Then the mind added music, resulting in an unimaginable world of sight and sound.

Sandra and Andrew were tall enough to stand next to the gas barrel and sniff. I was too short and needed to climb onto the barrel. The problem was getting off and usually I fell. I lost several teeth that summer. Fortunately, I felt no pain.

Our parents did everything they could to stop the practice. We would be sent to bed without dinner. The punishment however, was not very effective, given that in our world of color and sound, no one needed food. Occasionally, our mother would try to spank us. While the first offender was being punished (usually the oldest) the others would hide. On one occasion, Andrew and I hid in a full rain barrel. We simply stripped down and jumped in, completely naked. It had not occurred to us that our clothes would give away our whereabouts.

Dad would hammer shut the bungs on the barrels. We frantically tried to open them. If we were unsuccessful we would lie face down on the tractor with our noses in the gas tank. From my point of view, it only meant the fall was further.

Eventually winter came and it was cold. Gas does not evaporate well in cold weather so there were no fumes to sniff. By early winter our addiction was over. It was the only summer that my parents prayed for winter. It may however explain some of my subsequent behavior.

* * * * *

When I was still very young, my uncle ran over my head with a steel-wheeled wagon. There were three full barrels of gas on the flatbed wagon that was pulled by a tractor. My older brother and sister were able to jump directly onto the wagon. I could not because I was too small. I would have to climb. The wheels on the wagon were large, extending above the floor of the flatbed. I began to climb by using the spokes of the wheels. When I was almost able to step onto the wagon, my uncle started forward. I hung on to the wheel. My head was already over the top. As the wheel rotated I was upside down. My head hit the gravel ahead of the wheel, and was run over. There was blood everywhere.

My father scooped me up, shouted for my mother to come, and we were off to the hospital. I did not cry. My parents thought I was unconscious, but I heard every

6

word of their conversation. From time to time Mom would assure Dad that I was still breathing. Through tears they talked about what a good boy I was. They said that I was smart and sensitive; that if I lived they would surely take good care of me. They hoped that I still had a great future. Other than for the "if I lived" part, it was the most pleasant trip I had ever taken. Unfortunately, all good things end. My head healed, although that may be the subject of some debate among those who know me.

Some time thereafter, we were visiting another family. They had an old, scrawny, ill-tempered dog. While we were there the dog bit someone. The owner had had enough. He went out and killed the dog by striking it over the head with a hammer. He did not realize that I was standing nearby. I asked him why he killed the dog. He was clearly startled then he smiled and said, "What's it to you – you related?" He said it as a joke and I took it as such. Nevertheless, I was somewhat unsettled. I knew I wasn't good-looking. In fact, I knew that I was a scrawny, cross-eyed, buck-toothed kid with bad posture. But to be compared to that dog was a bit much.

Later that night we went home. Although I said nothing, Dad appeared to sense my unease. He invited me to sit in the front seat next to him. Seat belts were not required in those days. He put his arm around me and I slept. When we arrived home I woke up. His arm was still around me. It was then that I knew there was a place in this world for a bewildered five-year-old.

* * * * *

My pre-school years were wonderful. I loved my Dad. He was everything I wanted to be when I grew up and I told him so. I would do anything for him, and on one occasion I actually did.

One day a neighbor came over and he and Dad began to argue, I don't remember why. But how dare he? This was my dad and you don't talk to him like that. There wasn't much a kid could do, but I would do what I could. So, while he was arguing with my Dad, I stepped behind him and peed into his boots. Dad wasn't impressed but he didn't punish me either.

Then one day my world nearly stopped. I was about ten years old. There was a knock on the classroom door. The teacher went to answer. When she came back into the classroom she motioned for me to come. As I was leaving the classroom she put her arm around my shoulder and closed the door behind me. This can't be good, I thought. I was left in the hallway with the school secretary. I saw my mother standing in front of the Principal's office, wiping her eyes.

"Your father has been in an accident," the secretary said and then paused. I stopped breathing. He's dead, I thought. "And your mother is here to pick you up," she continued.

"Is he dead?" I asked in a thin, squeaky voice.

"Pardon."

I tried again. "Is he dead?"

"He's in the hospital," she said casually.

Although it had been only a few seconds, it seemed as though my world had gone into slow motion. It returned to normal once I started talking to my mother and she told me what happened.

Dad had been doing some custom harvesting on a neighboring farm. As was often the case, the farmers who finished their own harvest early would help those whose harvest was not yet done.

Dad had made a "blower," which was basically a wagon with a sloped floor. At the low end of the slope was a channel that guided the grain into a fan that then propelled the grain into the grain bins. A power-take-off-shaft ran from the tractor to the blower, which when engaged, would rotate the fan.

It was early in the morning and it had frozen the night before. Dad started up the tractor, engaged the power-take-off-shaft and throttled up. He slipped on the frost that had accumulated on the platform of the tractor and fell onto the power-take-off-shaft. The shaft caught his clothing.

My father was a large man. He was six feet four

9

inches tall, and weighed about 200 pounds. His body could not squeeze between the power shaft and the hitch of the wagon. As his clothing spun around the shaft, they first tightened around his body and then began to tear off. His left arm was also twisted around the shaft, and was torn out of its shoulder socket. With his other arm, he grabbed the hitch of the wagon and the tractor stalled. After he unwrapped himself from the shaft, he was virtually naked. The damage to his body was extensive. He had a dislocated left shoulder, and all his ribs on his left side were broken. He also had a deep laceration on his left leg.

The neighbor wrapped a blanket around him and drove him to our place. Mom then dressed him as best she could and drove him to the hospital, where he remained for several days. Ordinarily, our prayers were rote. We were usually too self-conscious to pray for personal things, but that evening we all prayed for Dad. Apart from some ongoing back pain, he recovered.

* * * * *

Although my father was a very tolerant person, he always insisted that we tell the truth. He would only become angry with us if we lied to him. However, if we told him the truth he would patiently help us work things out.

My mother was different. Although she was an

excellent mother and wife, she was impulsive, and occasionally quick to anger. She was a small woman and at an early age I was already taller than her.

On one occasion we argued, I do not remember why. After I left the house she followed me, and struck me on the back with a broom. I turned around, seized the broom and broke the handle over my knee. I then threw the two pieces over the garage.

My father was working in a field about one mile away. I walked over to him and told him about the argument and about what I had done. He thought awhile. He was clearly not pleased. "There are two issues," he said. "One is the argument, and the other is the broom. How do you intend to make it right?"

"I could say that I am sorry," I said.

"That's a start," he replied, "but she still doesn't have her broom back. You still have to make it right."

I thought about it. I had no money to buy another. "I can try to fix it," I said. When the handle broke, it had not broken across the shaft. Rather, it had split lengthways along the shaft.

I told my father about my plans. "Do what you can," he said. I went back to the yard, found the two parts of the broom and went to work.

The confrontation with my mother had occurred about mid-morning. At noon she brought lunch to my father in the field. I could see them talk. Eventually she returned to the house. That afternoon I avoided her.

In the meantime I had glued together the two pieces of the shaft. Because it takes a while for wood glue to set, I also strapped some tape around it. At the base of the shaft I wrote, "I'm sorry Mom. I love you. Winson."

When Dad returned in the late afternoon, I showed him what I had done and the words I had written. He nodded. "Have you apologized yet?" he asked.

"No," I replied.

"Then do that first," he said.

We walked into the house together. I told my mother how sorry I was. I gave her the broom. I showed her the words I had written. "Thank you," she said. But she never did use that broom. The next day she purchased another. I never saw that broom again.

* * * * *

As I got older I continued to seek my father's advice. When I was about eleven years old, my sister Sandra (who was two years older than I) invited her friend over for the weekend.

We had no running water at that time. Every Saturday evening everyone was expected to take a bath. Mom would boil water on the stove and pour the water into a tub which was already half full of cold water. She would continue to pour until the water reached the desired temperature. The tub was no more than 2½ feet in diameter. The girls always bathed first, then the boys. The same water was used but occasionally some hot water was added.

We had no indoor bathroom. The tub was always placed in a small room on top of a trap door that went to the basement. In the room were also coat hangers attached to the wall that were used by everyone. At one point I came in from outside and went into the room to hang my coat. There was my sister's friend — she was completely naked. She was standing in the tub drying herself. The towel was behind her back. I had never seen a naked girl before. It was clear, even to me, that she was well into puberty.

I ran out of the house. I wasn't sure what to do. I found my Dad and told him what had happened and what I had seen. "Should I apologize?"

Dad thought for a moment. "Did you like what you saw?" he asked.

"Well yes," I stammered.

"Good," he said. And that was the end of the matter.

* * * * *

I am not sure why I reacted the way I did. It wasn't as if I didn't know anything about sex. Being raised on a farm I soon learned where babies came from. In fact, I cannot remember not knowing.

My grandfather (on my mother's side) had a dairy farm. Most dairy farmers did not have bulls on their farms. Bulls were too dangerous, too unpredictable and too difficult to keep confined. However, my grandfather did have a bull. It was a massive beast. I have never seen a bull as large as that one. When it stood in the barn its back nearly touched the ceiling. Because of its size it was prized as a breeding bull.

It was always tied up, except for the many conjugal visits. Not much frightened me on the farm, but that bull did. It was always snorting, bellowing and banging the edges of the stanchions. My grandfather seemed to be the only person who could control it.

When the farmers needed their cows "serviced" they would transport the cows to my grandfather's farm. The procedure was always the same. The bull had a ring in its nose. My grandfather would attach a short pole to the ring and lead the bull out of the barn. Once they were outside, the farmer who owned the cow would attach a longer pole to the ring. My grandfather would then disconnect the shorter pole, take the longer pole and lead the bull to the cow.

Generally things worked out, but not always. The most dangerous part was getting the bull out of the barn. My grandfather would never allow anyone in the barn when the bull was being ushered out. We would watch from the trap door in the loft.

The principle behind controlling a bull is pain avoidance. Apparently a bull's nose is sensitive and when the ring is pulled it is very painful. If the bull was misbehaving, the ring was pulled tight. When it behaved the ring was allowed some slack.

On one occasion my grandfather was attempting to lead the bull outside. It was very rambunctious. My grandfather was a small man but he was quick on his feet. Although he could control the bull's head, its back end was swinging back and forth in a wide arch. There were a number of pillars in the barn that held up the floor of the loft. The bull's back end hit one of those pillars and dislodged it. Then it got itself backwards into one of the cow stalls and crushed the wooden manger as if it were kindling. I was watching in horror. The "safe" end of the bull was doing all the damage, and my grandfather was still on the "dangerous" end, with nothing to control it except a ring through the nose. I was certain my grandfather would not enjoy another birthday.

By the time the bull was outside, it was foaming at the mouth. Its eyes were blood red, and it was bellowing. The other farmer was supposed to attach his longer pole onto the ring but he was afraid. So my grandfather was left to hold the bull with his short pole. The bull then saw the cow and pain or no pain it was not to be denied. It dragged my grandfather along but when it mounted the cow my grandfather had to let go, because the pole was too short.

For the first time in its adult life this dangerous animal was free range. The farmer was hiding in his truck. I was sure that there would be nothing left standing in the yard. However when the bull dismounted, my grandfather quickly took hold of the short pole that was still dangling from the bull's nose and quietly walked it back to the barn. Thereafter I have always been fearful of bulls, and with some justification. Joyce's father and brother, both of whom are ranchers, have been severely injured by them.

At evening devotions my parents would occasionally ask us if there was a part of Scripture that we would like read. That evening I asked Dad to read the part about a horse that could be controlled by a small bit. I didn't know where to find it, but my mother did. It was James 3:3, and Dad read it: "When we put bits into the mouths of horses, to make them obey us, we can turn the whole animal." My parents looked perplexed, so I told them what had happened. It was a tribute to my grandfather.

When it was time for the cows to give birth, they would occasionally require assistance. Sometimes the problem was that the calf was breeched, that is, it was backwards in the birth canal, and sometimes the calf was too big. In either case, Dad was required to reach into the birth canal and assist the cow by pulling the calf out.

From time to time a mechanical device was used to pull. Even as a little boy I was often present and would help my Dad if necessary. Everything about procreation was as natural as breathing.

* * * * *

At that time, every farmer owned guns. My father owned two: an old shotgun and a .22 caliber rifle. Access to the guns was unrestricted; both guns were always in the garage, as was the ammunition. Even before grade school I had learned to use the "22." I did not use the shotgun because it was too heavy and "kicked" too much. My brother was older and stronger. Consequently, when we hunted together he used the shotgun and I had the "22." The nickname for the shotgun was "Touchy," because it had a hair trigger. If anything bumped it, however slightly, it would fire, unless the safe was on.

When my father first began raising chickens they were free-range. One summer we began to find dead chickens throughout the pasture, some partially eaten. We suspected a weasel, fox or coyote. My brother and I decided to hunt it down. The most likely hiding place would be under one of the many grain bins. They had all been built on skids and so there was ample room for an animal to hide.

We crawled along the grain bins and looked under.

At one point we found ourselves looking under the same grain bin at the same time, but from opposite sides. Eventually I thought I saw something move and I shot at it but whatever it was had disappeared. Perhaps it was hiding in a hole under the grain bin. I crawled under for a closer look. But there was nothing – not even a hole. Then I heard a hissing noise from somewhere on the other side and crawled back out to investigate. The bullet had gone through the tire of a disk that was standing some distance away. Unfortunately, we continued to find dead chickens, so we set out some traps. The next morning the culprit was caught. It was a beautiful horned owl.

* * * * *

The owl was not our only problem. In the fall of that year I was feeding the chickens by scattering wheat on the ground. I heard two shotgun blasts from a car that was passing by. Most of the chickens flew up but not all. Some were dead. I could see the blood. I picked one up and ran to the barn where Dad was working.

"Dad, someone shot our chickens," I shouted breathlessly.

He looked as shocked as I was. I quickly told him what happened.

"Which way did he go?" Dad asked.

"West," I answered.

What the shooter didn't know was that the road west of our place was a dead end. He had to come back the same way he went in. Dad quickly got into the car and parked it in the middle of the road. He then stood next to the car waiting for him to return. As expected, he did come back, but he didn't stop. He drove into the ditch and bypassed my Dad. Dad attempted to chase him but it was too late.

In the meantime, I ran to the end of the driveway near where Dad had parked because I wanted to see the confrontation. However, the shooter used the driveway to get his vehicle back on the road and in doing so, he nearly hit me. Fortunately, as he went by I memorized the license plate number. When Dad returned from the chase he called the police, giving them the number.

The following Sunday there was a knock on the door. It was the shooter. He had come to apologize. He acknowledged what he had done and said that we had every right to be upset with him. The police had come to see him. They told him that if he could make it right with the owner of the chickens and if the owner agreed to drop the charges, they would not arrest him. He owned a trucking company. If he were arrested and found guilty, he would lose his "bond," meaning that he could no longer carry on business. They talked for a long time. He seemed genuinely sorry and he paid for the damage.

Eventually Dad agreed that he would drop the charges. Because the shooter had endangered my life, I'm not sure that Dad was ever comfortable with that decision. I think not.

* * * * *

One fall evening my bother and I were preparing to go hunting because the ducks would soon be flying. We were in the garage and my brother was loading Touchy. One shell stuck in the magazine so he slammed the butt of the gun on the floor to dislodge the shell. He had forgotten the bullet in the firing chamber. The gun fired and blew a hole through the ceiling of the garage and out the roof. I had been standing nearby. After the shot neither of us could hear anything, except for some ringing.

We saw Dad running to the garage. We did not want him to see the damage so we met him outside. His lips were moving, but we heard nothing. We tried to lip read and said, "Yes Dad," as often as we thought necessary. Eventually, he went back into the house and we attempted to repair the damage.

Unfortunately, my parents had guests that evening. They had been visiting for some time. The wife was pregnant. Shortly after the incident, the guests left. We later learned that the shot had severely startled them. The lady was particularly upset because she thought she was having a miscarriage.

* * * * *

Our only contact with the broader world was through radio. We had only one radio, and with ten people in the house, the demand for radio time was high. Every Thursday evening there was a program called "Famous Jury Trials" which aired for a number of years. Every person in our home had his or her favorite program, and this was mine.

Each story was different but all were true. I was fascinated. These were real trials conducted by real lawyers. Whatever else I was doing would be interrupted so I could listen. My parents knew how much I enjoyed these programs and they were accommodating. Consequently, every Thursday evening would see me huddled in front of the radio, listening.

Eventually, the program was no longer aired. By that time however, I knew that more than anything else, I wanted to be a trial lawyer. Many years later, I phoned various radio stations in Edmonton and asked about the programs. I was hoping to get the recordings, but no one seemed to remember the programs, let alone find them.

* * * * *

On our farm, water was always an issue, especially in the summer when the demand for water was high. Our well was very deep and reliable but the number of gallons per minute taken from the well was limited. As a result, in the summer Andrew and I were required to haul water from our neighbor's man-made pond called a "dug-out." It was located adjacent to a creek. We used our tractor to pull a 300-gallon water tank that was mounted on a two-wheeled cart. We would back the cart as close to the dugout as we dared and then fill the tank, one pail-full at a time.

The work was difficult, but we didn't mind, because when the weather was warm we would go swimming. Also, the area next to the creek must have been the site of a Native American camp and we would often spend our time collecting arrowheads. Unfortunately we had no way of knowing how valuable the arrowheads were and none were saved.

The creek flowed into a very shallow lake. The entire area was muskeg. As such, there was no real bottom to either the creek or the lake and when we stepped on the bottom we slowly kept sinking.

One warm fall day I decided to take the shotgun. I planned to do some hunting after I had filled the water tank because I knew that there were some ducks and geese on the lake. I had taken my hip-waders. After filling the water tank I put on the hip-waders and stood in the bulrushes at the edge of the lake. From time to time I would shoot at a flock of ducks or geese as they flew overhead. Finally one goose came down. I could tell that its wing was broken and I walked into the lake to retrieve it but the goose was not dead. As I walked toward it, it swam further out. I tried to shoot it on the water but it was always out of range.

After I shot the goose, its mate continued to fly in circles over the injured goose. Both were honking back and forth to each other. At first I tried to shot the mate but it was flying too high.

By the time I realized I was in trouble, I was nearly in the middle of the lake. Whenever I stopped, I began to sink so I had to keep going. I began to feel faint, as I was getting overheated. I kept splashing water on my face. I tried to remove the hip-waders but the pressure of the water on the waders made it impossible. Further, when I lifted one leg to remove the waders, the other foot sank even more quickly. Eventually the waders filled with water, making mobility even more difficult.

I tried to keep the shotgun out of the water, but my arms became too tired. Finally I put the gun into one of the pant-legs of the waders, but not so deep that I could not bend my knee. I tried to swim but I was exhausted. I was trying hard to save myself, but I was sure that I was losing.

I began to pray, or more specifically, I began to make promises. I promised God that if he saved me I would always obey Him and do His will. I cannot remember what the other promises were, but I know that at the time I was sincere. It is probably just as well that I cannot remember, because I am quite sure that I kept none of them.

There was one point in particular when I thought my time had come. I had stopped to rest. The water was up to my shoulders, and I was faint. When I tried to move, my feet were stuck. I was gradually sinking deeper and deeper. The only way to lift one leg, was to force the other down, which meant that I was sinking faster than if I did nothing. But doing nothing was not an option. I worked my feet as hard as I could. By this time the water was around my neck and desperation set in. Finally I broke free, but I knew that I could not stop again. Slowly I made my way to shore. I lay on the ground and took off the hip-waders. I never wore them again. Years later I gave them to a friend.

As I was recuperating on the shore I watched the two geese interact. They continued to look and honk at each other. The mate seemed to be tying to get the injured goose to fly. After I was no longer in the lake, the mate landed next to the injured goose. Now they were no longer honking. Rather they were urgently gabbling.

They touched each other's bills in a show of affection. Then the mate would nudge the injured goose and run on the water as if it were about to fly. It was trying to encourage the other to leave. Eventually it seemed to accept that its injured mate could not fly and together they swam away.

That night and for many nights thereafter I dreamt about the geese. Every night I could hear the mournful honking of this committed pair. It became a recurring nightmare.

* * * * *

My aunt Alice (a sister to my mother) had been a missionary in Suriname (formerly called Dutch Guiana) and had worked in the southern rain forests with a particular tribe. That tribe believed that if the eldest son died, it meant that the gods were angry with the parents. In that circumstance it was necessary for the parents to sacrifice the second son to appease the angry gods.

In one case a first-born son died in childbirth, which was not unusual. Eventually, a second son was born. Notwithstanding the death threats from some local tribesmen, my aunt persuaded the parents to allow her to adopt him. She called him "Winson," after the same grandfather that I was named after. He was a year or two younger than me. She taught him to speak English, along with Dutch (which was the official language of Suriname.) When he was a teenager she brought him to visit us. His skin was a copper color.

Throughout the entire visit he said virtually nothing. He appeared to be shy in the extreme. We tried to engage him in all sorts of activities but he usually just shook his head. He seemed to want nothing more than to be left alone. Even my aunt became more and more exasperated with him.

It was time to haul water from the dugout. I asked him if he wanted to go swimming. He nodded but said nothing. I was surprised. He came onto the tractor with me but despite my best efforts to engage him in conversation, he said nothing. I was getting more and more frustrated. Why wouldn't he say anything? I decided to ignore him.

When we arrived at the dugout, I filled the tank. Then I walked to the creek, removed all my clothes and went swimming as I normally did. When I was done, I dressed, but Winson was nowhere to be seen. I called his name, but there was no response. I started up the tractor thinking that the noise might attract him. Again there was no response. I was becoming concerned and began to look for him.

Eventually, I found his clothes neatly stacked behind some bushes, but he was gone. I assumed that he had gone swimming, so I began to look for him in the water. Because the creek flowed though muskeg the water was always brown and it was impossible to see more than a couple of inches below the surface. I ran back and forth along the shore calling his name but there was only silence. I was frantic. I was afraid he might have drowned, so I again took off my clothes and jumped back in. I was swimming back and forth feeling the bottom of the creek with my feet and the sides with my hands but I felt nothing.

I finally started walking back and forth along the far shore. Then I saw him, lying face up in the brown water. At first I thought he was dead, but then I noticed that his eyes were following me. I could not see him from the near shore because of the sun's reflection on the water. However from the far shore his face, which was above the water, was readily visible. Further, he was perfectly camouflaged in the brown water. When I spotted him, he came out of the water and dressed but he could not stop laughing. He told me that he had been watching me the whole time. I was not amused. In fact I was angry. He had remained hidden for almost an hour as I tried to find him.

On the way home he found his voice. He said that in Suriname they often played hide and seek in the rivers. He also said that he knew I couldn't see him because of the way the sun was shining. The more he laughed and gloried in his accomplishments the angrier I became. On

27

the way home it was I who wasn't talking.

Winson eventually became the governor of the entire district of which his tribe was a part. Needless to say the second sons are no longer sacrificed to appease the gods. But for the intervention of my aunt, Winson would not have lived.

* * * * *

When I was about thirteen or fourteen years old, my parents decided to visit my uncle and aunt and their family. They lived near Edson, Alberta, approximately two hours away. I was permitted to drive; Dad was in the passenger seat and Mom was in the back seat directly behind me. They had decided to take five-dozen eggs, contained in two flats. The eggs were on the back seat directly behind Dad.

We were on a gravel road, and on several occasions Dad had told me to slow down. As we approached a bridge, I noticed that the bridge deck was rounded. It looked like a giant speed bump. Because I was already so close to the bridge, I had to brake hard but the timing was unfortunate. The bridge deck catapulted the car upward. At the same time my braking propelled the items in the vehicle forward. The net result was that the eggs hit the roof of the car and landed on my Dad. Most of the eggs had broken when they hit the roof and were dripping on him. I looked his way. All I could see were two eyes and a mouth. The mouth was moving. I cannot remember what he said, but I assume he didn't approve of my driving.

Fortunately Mom was there. Every time she looked at Dad she burst out laughing. She tried not to, but she could not help herself. She was like a little girl who couldn't stop laughing during a prayer. Eventually, Dad did find some humor in it, albeit not much.

* * * * *

I am now thankful that during my teen years my Dad was firm but fair. He intuitively seemed to know when to be harsh and when to let lesser sins slide. Only once do I remember being angry with him. It was a Saturday morning and he told me that I could play hockey that afternoon. However, after feeding the hogs, he realized there was insufficient feed for the balance of the week so he told me that I could only play hockey after we had ground some grain for the pigs. I knew that would take most of the afternoon. I was furious. I had very much wanted to play.

The grain was ground by a hammer mill, powered by a tractor. A large flat belt ran from the hammer mill to the tractor. I tightened the belt as tightly as possible and started up the hammer mill. We mixed the grains.

Dad provided the barley from one side and I provided the wheat and supplement from the other. When he wasn't looking, I opened the little gate to the hammer mill as wide as possible. Then I took a five-gallon pail of wheat and threw it as hard as I could into the mill. The belt screamed and came off the pulleys, but continued to rotate around my Dad's head like some devil-possessed snake. It could easily have killed him. I cried most of the afternoon. I knew that the man I most admired was now profoundly disappointed in me.

* * * * *

When I was about fifteen or sixteen I decided to go hunting with three friends. I had spoken to my cousin in Edson, Alberta, and he told me that there were always deer on their property. They were happy to have hunters because the deer were damaging some of the crops. We could stay at their place and he would join us in the hunt.

It was winter and frightfully cold. On the day of the hunt it was -45 degrees Fahrenheit; nonetheless, we ventured out. My three friends decided to hunt as a group. I realized that if I stayed with them we would end up with nothing because they often shouted to each other. Also, because of the cold temperature, the snow crackled loudly when we walked. My cousin and I reasoned that the deer would hear them as well, so we went our separate ways.

I had learned from my father that when you hunt you must allow the deer to come to you. The best thing is to be both motionless and silent. And so I was when a deer crossed not more than 80 feet ahead of me. When I raised my rifle to shoot, I noticed that snow had lodged on the front sight. I slowly turned the gun around to blow the snow off the sight. The deer remained where it was. The wind was in my face and therefore the deer could not smell me.

When I turned the gun around I noticed that there was also snow in the barrel of the gun. I had no idea how much snow was in the barrel, nor did I know how tightly it was packed in. It may even have been ice. I was afraid that if I shot, the barrel might blow apart. I had read a story once about someone who deliberately packed used chewing gum into the barrel of a gun. When fired, the barrel blew apart injuring the shooter, although the intent had been to kill him.

In any event, I then did something incomprehensibly stupid. I decided to suck the snow and ice out of the barrel. I put the barrel of the loaded gun into my mouth. To my surprise my lips instantly froze to the barrel. In hindsight, it would probably have been better to endure the pain and pull the gun out of my mouth, but it takes time to consider the options. I took off one glove and tried to warm the barrel with my hand, but it didn't work. I only succeeded in freezing my hand. By now, pulling the gun out of my mouth was no longer an option. My mouth was more fully frozen to the barrel than before. I turned the gun to the side so that if it fired it would only blow out my cheek. I then reached out and flicked the safety on.

I had been hiding behind a cluster of thick thorn bushes. The thorns had caught a number of dry leaves. Back then many teenagers smoked, including me so I always carried a lighter in my pocket. With one hand I managed to bundle up the thorn bushes and the leaves and start a fire. Then with my head on the ground I laid the barrel of the gun across the fire, with my face as close to the fire as possible. Gradually, the barrel of the gun heated up enough to enable me to take it out of my mouth. Other than some soreness I was okay, as was the deer.

* * * * *

Every teenager wants to be accepted and admired. I was fairly pleased with who I was except for one thing. I have an awful sounding laugh and I was afraid that someone would ridicule me because of it. Most people laugh when they exhale. I laugh when I inhale. The result is, that I sound like a horse neighing backwards. I have always disliked the sound so I don't laugh very much, at least not out loud.

When I was about sixteen years old I decided to change my laugh. I had heard a laugh once that I liked. It was a from-the-chest ha, ha. I practiced for months. It sounded like the lovely baritone deep-throated laugh I always wanted.

One Sunday evening, after Young People's Society, we had a party at our home. At one point someone told a joke. I had been waiting for an opportunity. Now would be a good time to use it. "Ha, ha, ha" I laughed. There was dead silence. Everyone turned my way and stared in disbelief. Finally one of the girls said, "Ha, ha, ha to you too." I felt totally embarrassed, but now was not the time to flinch.

"Do you want to hear it again?" I asked. Some said "yes," others said "no."

"Ha, ha, ha" I laughed again. By now most people thought I was trying to make a joke, so the matter was dropped. No one knew how hard I had worked to perfect it. For a while I was gripped with fear every time I was with the same group. I was afraid that someone would ask me to do the "ha, ha" laugh again, but no one did.

Eventually I came to accept that I am who I am, laugh and all. I could have avoided some fear and embarrassment if I had simply accepted my mother's advice. "Accept who you are. Don't try to be the same as others, when you were created to be different."

33

* * * * *

Humility is a virtue that is difficult for teenagers to accept. When I was eighteen or nineteen, I worked for my brother in law, Henry Strydhorst. He was a carpenter and we were building a barn for Simon Tuininga. Toward the end of the summer Henry and Simon were discussing the next summer's project, which I believe was to build another barn. I was standing nearby.

Simon asked Henry if he could get enough help to build the next barn. I had not told Henry that I would not be available the following summer, and I didn't want him to think that he could rely on me.

"I won't be here next year," I said.

Simon looked at me. "You're not indispensable," he replied.

For a long time I thought about what Simon said. It was obviously true, but I found it hard to accept. What it meant was that I was dispensable. If I died, I would simply be replaced. Most people wouldn't even notice. I realized that I had not yet done anything that even those close to me could remember me by. Simon's words, perhaps more than any other have stayed with me. Even today it makes me a little sad, especially when I consider that I am closer to being replaced now than I was then. Eventually, someone else will occupy the space I now occupy. Others will live in the home I now live in.

* * * * *

I left home for college when I was twenty. When I look back, I realize how fortunate I was. I am thankful for my parents. I know I was a difficult child, but together they steered me through. I am thankful for my Dad, for the time we spent together and for the lessons he taught me. I now know that when I do wrong, an apology is important, but it is not enough. I must make it right. To the extent possible, I must undo the wrong.

He taught me the value of truth, patience and tolerance. Without truth, no relationship is possible. I am so very thankful that he was accepting of me, and that he listened to me. When I most needed it, he gave me the assurance that there was a place in this world for me.

I am thankful for my Mother. She always insisted that whenever possible the entire family have dinner together. She made every effort to make that happen. Saturday evenings were always special. Through my mother I learned the value of education. She encouraged me to persevere and to see a task through to completion. She taught me to be responsible, to be organized and to be focused.

I am thankful that I grew up in a large family. There was always someone to play with or to talk to. I am thankful that we did not have television. I am especially thankful for my older brother Andrew. He always included me. When we were young we had our fights but over the years he has been my best friend.

CHAPTER 2

SCHOOL DAYS

I had always wanted to be a trial lawyer. Why I became a pastor instead is explained in this chapter. From grades one through ten, I attended the Neerlandia School. In effect it was a Christian school in the public school system. The school board members that governed the school were all Christians from the local church. My father was often a member of the board. All the teachers were also Christians.

Grade school was easy for me. Two others in my class and I completed grades three and four in one year. The effect was that the next year we advanced to grade five. Some of the other parents complained. They thought it odd that three students from one class should all advance at once. Others thought their children were just as talented as we were and should also advance. Still others wondered what the payoff had been.

Our teacher promoted our advancement and the principal supported her. Eventually the issue came before the Superintendent of Schools. He reversed the decision and ordered that we be placed back in grade four. The problem was that we had already done grade four and we had excelled. The teacher did her best to challenge us but eventually gave up. She had been given strict instructions not to attempt to advance us again. In fact the Superintendent then developed a policy that he imposed on all schools. "In the best interest of all children, no child's advancement will be accelerated."

Several times a day we would be excused from class. We spent a great deal of time in the gym. The teacher had attempted to use us as a teacher's assistant; however, our classmates resented it and their parents complained. As a result, we lost interest in the curriculum. Worse still, we lost our place in class. Before, we were the academic leaders of our class and we were admired for it. We were motivated to excel. Now, we were resented.

My father did the best he could to rectify the situation, but to no avail.

Eventually we re-entered the social mix but our status had changed. We could no longer be the academic leaders. In fact, of the three of us, I was the only one who continued after high school.

I became a fun loving, mischievous teenager with a talent for public speaking and I was accepted as such.

* * * * *

Once a year, the community nurse would show a film to the fifth grade girls. While the film was shown the boys were sent outside. Notwithstanding our best efforts, the girls never told us what the film was about. And so the challenge arose. I was determined to find out but it would not be easy. The film was shown in the gym with the doors locked.

A very large furnace heated our school. It was centrally located in the basement with an enormous cold air duct running from the gym to the furnace.

This was our ticket to the movies. My friend and I removed the filters and crawled through the cold air duct to the gym. It was a considerable distance. When we arrived under the gym we were met with a large grate that covered the duct. We lifted the grate that we had previously loosened and began watching the film.

Because we had not seen the movie from the beginning it was a bit confusing. It was about a girl who, because of some condition, found she could not go swimming. We were fascinated.

At some point, several girls noticed that they were not alone. They immediately found a tumbling mat and placed it over the grate. They then sat on the mat. Our gig was up. Fortunately, it was dark and they had not recognized us. We crawled back and cleaned ourselves up. Notwithstanding the teacher's best efforts, we were never found out.

* * * * *

In grade six our classroom was next to the teachers' room. At that time classes lasted one hour. At the end of each hour an inside bell was rung. Also at the beginning and end of each day an outside bell was rung. The buttons for both bells were located in the teachers' room. Every day the sixth grade teacher would ask a student to ring the last bell.

Although we referred to the buttons as bells, each had its own sound. The inside bell sounded like a siren. The outside bell sounded like a ship's horn. One day the teacher asked me to ring the bells. On my way into the teachers' room I met my friend who was just returning from the washroom. I asked him to help me ring the bells. We agreed that he would ring the outside bell and I would ring the inside. We further agreed that we would do the Morse code on the bells. We locked ourselves into the teachers' room, and so it began.

We were not sure how the Morse code went, so we practiced. My friend thought it was two longs and one short. I though it was one long, a short and a long. We practiced both. Soon the teacher was at the door demanding that we open it. She said we would be expelled from school for what we were doing. Then the principal came and the message was the same; we would be expelled.

Our position was: if we were going to be expelled anyway, why would we open the door? We offered to stop the bells and open the door if they agreed not to punish us. When they refused we practiced some more. Eventually they agreed. We would not be punished if we stopped ringing the bells and opened the door. There were two conditions. We were not to tell our classmates and we were to apologize. We agreed and opened the door. They kept their agreement and we kept ours.

We learned later that at least one person had been inconvenienced as a result of the bell ringing. In one class, once a week the last half hour of the day was devoted to religious instruction. The minister from the local church conducted classes and always concluded the class with the Lord's Prayer.

When the first bell rang the minister said, "That will be all for today – let's pray. Our Fath..." there were two long sirens, and one short.

He waited, and then started again. "Our Fath..." there was one long, one short and another long siren.

He waited, and then started again. "Our Fath..."

41

now there was an assortment of sirens.

And so it went. Finally the minister said "enough" and left.

In spite of the bell ringing, I had a good relationship with the teacher. My apology was sincere. I truly liked my teacher and she liked me. I felt awful for what I had done. Prior to this I had done some undesirable things but I had never harmed or embarrassed anyone. Especially not someone I liked. The bell ringing had started on impulse and through hubris had grown into something ugly. Thereafter, I tried to make up for my one act of insubordination in whatever way I could.

* * * * *

Grades 11 and 12 were done at the Barrhead High School, some fifteen miles away. I was only interested in sports, nothing else, and my grades reflected this. The high school had a football program that I was interested in. Unfortunately, most of the games were played on Sunday and my parents would never allow me to do anything on Sunday, let alone play football. Sunday was for worship.

Over time I developed a plan. Our worship services were in the morning and early afternoon. The games were played late in the afternoon or early evening. I needed my parents' car, because I didn't have my own.

I told them that I wanted to date a particular girl. I knew my parents liked her. I further told them that I wanted to take this girl to her church service which was in the late afternoon. My parents seemed quite happy with this arrangement. It meant that I would attend three worship services. More was better.

And so it was that many Sundays I drove to Barrhead and played football. I played defense and consequently my name never appeared in the local paper. After the games I drove to the girl's church. Their worship service was over and usually the church was vacant. I would then pick up the Sunday Bulletin for proof of attendance and return home.

Toward the end of the football season, a problem arose. My parents insisted that I invite my girlfriend for Sunday dinner. In fact, we had never dated at all.

Nonetheless, I decided to invite her. If she refused I would tell my parents that we had broken up. She accepted and although there were some awkward moments, no one was the wiser. After football season I told my parents that we had split up.

* * * * *

My grades reflected my interests. They were not good. Certainly not good enough to go to university, let alone law school. My parents were deeply disappointed in me.

43

They had seen my potential. They told me to find a job but the only jobs available were in the lumber industry so I took a job working in a sawmill. I lived and worked in a company camp located miles into the bush.

After the logs were harvested, they were brought into camp. Each log was then placed on a carriage that pushed it through the saw. The carriage operator would always square the log first. That meant that the first four cuts were to remove the slabs. The slab is the rounded part of the log that was cut off, essentially the bark. My job was to remove the slabs and throw them onto the slab pile. The slabs were long and heavy. Often they would break, meaning that there were now three or four shorter slabs to remove.

The saw was very noisy. We were required to wear earplugs, but they didn't help very much. My ears would ring all night. When the saw was not operational, I would go into the bush with the other loggers and cut down or de-limb the trees. I preferred the work in the bush.

In the summer, life in camp was an adventure; in the winter however, life was very difficult. We often worked in −30 degree weather. The workers were snarly, and the company demanding. Bad weather, snow or frozen vehicles often cut off home visits. About mid-winter, I came to a certain realization – this life was not for me. Many of the older loggers had also started logging after high school. They hated the work but were unable to find anything else. Some were constantly complaining.

I had seen lives unfulfilled. Many of the loggers were clearly talented people. One loved to sing and was an exceptional singer. Unless he found a way to become what he wanted to be, he would die with the songs we should have heard, still within him. It was a waste, not because logging is not a worthy vocation, but because it wasn't what he wanted to do.

I had matured in the bush. Life was hard and it had a sobering effect on my attitude. While in the bush, I had the opportunity to evaluate my life. I thought about the values my parents had attempted to instill in me. I realized that life was more than fun and frolic. I began to appreciate the value of learning. More and more, I was becoming the person I was before grade four. My life needed purpose and what greater purpose was there than to preach the gospel. I told my parents that I wanted to become a pastor. They were delighted. Their Christian faith was very important to them. To have a son who promoted Christianity was priceless.

While in high school I had won an international oratorical contest. Our denomination had developed a program whereby young speakers competed against each other. There were four levels of competition: local, regional, national and international. I won at every level. As a result my parents had encouraged me to become a pastor. Now they thought that their prodigal son had gone straight and in many ways I had.

However my new resolve to become a pastor did not begin well. Soon everyone in the community knew that I wanted to become a pastor. Every Sunday evening we had young people's society. One Sunday I was asked to close the meeting with prayer. Back then prayers did not sound like they do today. The old English was always used. For example a prayer might begin as follows: "Our Father, we love thee because thou art great and greatly to be praised." Needless to say, not many prayers were offered in the bush and certainly not in old English. It wasn't long before I was completely confused by the "thees, thous and therefores." Further, by concentrating on the words, I had forgotten the subject matter. I had truly lost the forest for the trees. I stood in silence for a long time. Eyes were opening, until everyone was staring at me. The weight of silence became unbearable and then my brother Andrew suddenly stood up and said, "Amen." Everyone laughed, but the acute pain was over. I was only left with chronic embarrassment.

CHAPTER 3
COLLEGE AND SEMINARY

Dordt College

I was accepted by Dordt College, which is a liberal arts college. It is located in Sioux Center, a small town in the northwest corner of Iowa. The college offered a four-year pre-seminary program in which I enrolled.

It was during this time that I met an intelligent and very attractive Christian girl. Her name was Joyce Uiterdyk.

**Joyce-when we first met and the
Uiterdyk family ranch as it then was**

There is absolutely nothing as invigorating as young love. There is also nothing more time consuming. After three years of love, lust and longing, we married. The flame continues to sputter to this day. Marriage was marvelous. My parents gave us their used car. My uncle bought all my books. We had wonderful friends. Life was good.

Even though the decision to become a pastor was born out of desperation, it had become very real. I accepted without question that I would be a pastor. Acceptance brought contentment.

While attending college I also worked part-time. During the week I worked for an individual who owned a variety store. My job was to stock the shelves and keep inventory. The work was done in the evening after the store was closed.

On weekends I worked for various farmers. The work ranged from feeding cattle to cleaning corncribs. The corncribs were always infested with rats. The local farmers had developed an effective means of extermination. When the cribs were almost empty we were instructed to put a running lawn mower at the opening of the gutter. The gutter was cut into the floor of the crib. When the rats were no longer able to hide in the corn, they would try to escape through the gutter. By doing so they ran into the blades of the lawn mower.

During the summers I worked for Joyce's parents who farmed near Bozeman, Montana, which is located in the Gallatin Valley, surrounded by mountains. It is truly a scenic part of the world. Because of the mountains, rainfall is somewhat limited. During the first summer, Joyce's father and I installed a gravity-fed irrigation system that continues to be operational to this day.

* * * * *

Joyce and I were married on August 10, 1966. She had already been teaching in a Christian school in Ireton, Iowa for two years. Her school was about fifteen miles from Sioux Center. I had completed my third year of college.

The wedding was held in the First Christian Reformed Church, built on a hill in Joyce's hometown in Montana. The views are splendid. It was and continues to be, a large and beautiful church with lovely stained glass windows. It also has an exceptionally large pipe organ. The pipes formed a majestic background behind the elevated pulpit. It was the church where Joyce had worshipped with her family since she was an infant.

In that community a tradition had arisen whereby a number of young adults would chase down a newly married couple and prank them. Word was that one couple had been separated and placed on two trains going in opposite directions. We heard that something was planned for us. We later learned that they had planned to tie us to a sign on the highway which read "Welcome to Bozeman." They thought this would be appropriate for me as I was not from the community.

For our first night we had chosen a hotel in Bozeman with a honeymoon suite. It was a large, well-decorated room with a circular bed. Prior to the wedding we had hidden our car in Joyce's grandmother's garage which was located near the hotel.

During the wedding reception we told a few people that Vic Maris would be driving us to our honeymoon suite. Vic was a friend of mine from Peers, Alberta and owned a bright yellow muscle-car. We did not tell anyone where the honeymoon suite was. At about 11:00

p.m., and on cue, he left. Immediately the chase was on. He took the highway towards West Yellowstone Park, a favorite destination for honeymooners.

In the meantime, we had arranged to be driven to our suite by Diana and Bob Batch. Diana was Joyce's second cousin and Bob was a police officer in Helena, Montana. The car was an unmarked four-door sedan. Shortly after we left the church, Bob radioed the Bozeman police and asked them to secure the hotel entrances. He told them that he was transporting a newly married couple to their honeymoon suite. When we arrived at the hotel, police cars with lights flashing secured each entrance. We slowly made our way to the hotel suite, making sure we waved our thanks to each police vehicle. After we entered the suite, the police left.

Shortly thereafter we noticed that someone was trying to get into the room. We could see the door handle move. When the intruders could not get in they banged on the door a few times, then left. We later learned that the intruders were the people who had chased Vic Maris. In their vehicle was a police scanner so they had heard Bob's call for assistance. They knew where we were but it was too late.

On the day we were married, our friends Merle and Carol Buwalda were also married in Lynden, Washington. Merle had been a roommate of mine at Dordt College. Two days after our weddings, we met them in Lynden.

The four of us then drove in Merle's car to Abbotsford, B.C. to attend the wedding of Adrian and Pat Van Heyst. Adrian had also been a roommate of mine. They were clearly surprised to see us. They had assumed that all four of us would be enjoying our honeymoon elsewhere.

Later that evening we crossed back into the U.S. At the border crossing I realized that I had left all identifying documents in my car, which was still in Lynden. I had no way of proving that I was who I said I was. As expected, the customs agent asked for the documents. I explained to him that we were on our honeymoon, and that I had forgotten the documents, which were still in Lynden. He looked at the four of us in the car. Then he smiled, "I understand," he said pleasantly. "You obviously have other things on your mind." He then motioned us through.

* * * * *

That fall we returned to Sioux Center for my final year. We had previously arranged to rent a furnished suite through the college. The suite was the back half of the second floor of what had previously been called the "Grootenhuis dorm." In fact, the year before, the entire second floor had housed fourteen female students. Joyce had lived there in her freshman year.

Dale and Eleanor Grootenhuis and their family

lived downstairs. Dale was a professor at Dordt and conducted the senior choir. They were absolutely wonderful people. We often had occasion to babysit their boys.

During the summer the second floor had been divided, so that there were now two suites suitable for married couples. The back suite had been reserved for us. When we arrived, there was no furniture. We went to the college and spoke to the person responsible. He said that the renovations had just been completed, and that they had not had time to furnish it. However, he said that he would immediately deliver some bunk beds from the dorm.

We told him that we were just married and that bunk beds were not exactly what we had in mind. He said that he would see what he could do. We were later told that he had gone to a used furniture store, and the next day our suite was furnished and the furnishings included a double bed. It turned out that the suite was perfect for us.

The summer after my graduation from Dordt, Joyce and I lived in a little house in Bozeman. We took some courses at Montana State University; Joyce's courses were in education and mine were in philosophy. When not in class, I worked for Joyce's dad. Life continued to be good. The next step would be the seminary which is where the real training to become a pastor would begin.

Calvin Theological Seminary

Calvin Theological Seminary

After four years of college I graduated and enrolled into Calvin Theological Seminary, located in Grand Rapids, Michigan. For most seminarians, classes started in September. However, for first-year students, classes began in mid-August. It was an intensive, every day, all day, two-week course in Hebrew. The purpose was to learn to read the Bible in the original language.

Prior to moving to Grand Rapids, we had arranged to stay in a home that was leased by Adrian and Pat Van Heyst. Adrian was a second year seminarian, so his classes did not begin until September. The home was vacant because the Van Heysts were in Grande Prairie, Alberta, serving in a church there for the summer. They had mailed us the keys. The home would be available to us for two weeks. This would enable us to find suitable accommodation. Joyce was pregnant at the time.

We arrived in Grand Rapids in late afternoon, went directly to the home and opened the door with the keys that had been sent to us. We were surprised to find another couple living there. They said the Van Heysts had given them permission but the Van Heysts denied this.

There was not enough room for two couples. We phoned some other friends and stayed there for the night. Most rental accommodation is available at the end of the month and we had arrived in mid-August. Even though there was little available, we found an unfurnished suite the next day. That night we slept on the floor.

The suite consisted of the top floor in a two-storey house. We soon learned why the suite was vacant. At night the cockroaches lived there. We sprayed an insecticide but this simply drove the cockroaches to the main floor. The main floor occupants would then spray, driving the cockroaches back up.

Finally, with the main floor tenants, we managed to get the landlord to agree to fumigate both suites at the same time. This meant that we would have to vacate the property for twenty-four hours, which we did. When we got back, there were dead cockroaches everywhere.

* * * * *

Shortly after we arrived in Grand Rapids, both Joyce and I were able to find jobs at Pine Rest Christian Hospital. At that time it was the largest private mental health hospital in the United States. In addition to treating mental health patients, the hospital trained nurses. Joyce became a matron in the nurses' residence, working evening and night shifts.

I was hired full-time to work as a counselor on the teen ward. The ward was located in a three-storey building with geriatric patients occupying the upper two levels. The lower level was divided into two wards. The north ward was occupied by teenage girls; the south ward by teenage boys. Each ward housed twelve patients. Between the wards was a large kitchen and dining room that serviced all levels.

As was the case with Joyce, I also worked evenings and nights; however, our schedules were not always the same. Consequently, if Joyce worked nights and I was not working, I would go to the nurses' residence. Joyce would put me up in a vacant bedroom and I would stay the night. The nurses had no idea what their matron was up to.

Working on the teen ward was enormously interesting. Our job description was varied. We counseled, we cleaned, we kept order, we drove patients to various places and events, and we refereed or coached their games. At the end of the shift we recorded everything.

Twice a week the entire staff met with the psychiatrists and therapists who had patients on the ward. Each patient was discussed. Most of the patients were admitted to the hospital by their parents. Some were there by Court order. These patients usually had behavior problems and were occasionally violent.

One night I heard a patient quietly slip into the bathroom. This was unusual. Generally, the patients made no effort to mitigate noise. I decided to check things out so I walked into the bathroom. One of the court-ordered patients was combing his hair. He was fully dressed. He was over six feet tall and weighed about two hundred pounds. However, he was not athletic. In fact, he was somewhat clumsy.

I asked him what he was doing. He told me that he was going to California along with some of his friends. He also told me that they planned to go by taking my car. A confrontation seemed inevitable but I did not want it to happen in the bathroom. I bolted for the door that opened into a hallway. Just as I passed through the door the patient jumped onto my back, causing me to bend forward. Another two patients were waiting in the hallway, one holding what looked like a sawed-off baseball bat. Just as I was coming through the door he brought the bat down. His intent was to strike me on the head. He did not see his friend on my back and struck his friend squarely on the neck.

In the confusion, I was able to get away. My goal was to get to the nurses' station. It was long and narrow, no wider than a door. If I could get to the station and close the door, I would be safe. If I could not close the door then at least only one patient could approach me at a time.

Located in the hallway, between the bathroom and the nurses' station, was a newly installed emergency alarm system consisting of both sound and lights. It had not been used before. It was designed in such a way that – through a system of lights – all the caregivers in the building could tell who needed help. For example, if the lowest south light came on, it meant that I needed help.

On my dash to the nursing station I activated the alarm system by breaking a protective glass cover. I was shocked by how loud it was. It sounded like an air horn. Almost immediately the nurse from the girls' side came through the door. She was a tall athletic woman and looked very much like the big nurse in the movie, "One Flew Over the Cuckoo's Nest."

As soon as she came through the door, she ordered the patients to line-up and drop their pants which they did. She then gave them an injection in the buttocks and they were locked in a seclusion room.

In the meantime, I noticed another light on the

emergency board indicating a problem on the second floor directly above me. We immediately went up. All the patients on the second floor were elderly men, many of whom had served in the Second World War. Some may even have served in the First. It was 2:00 a.m. and they were all asleep when the obtrusive alarm sounded and it had terrified and confused them.

Today it may not be politically correct, and I mean no disrespect, but at the time there were three categories of patients on the second floor. There were the wheelies, the veggies, and the chronics. The wheelies were those who required a wheelchair; the veggies were bed-bound; and the chronics were those who stood motionless for hours. They were like sentries or snipers in an army, which perhaps they had been.

When we arrived on the second floor there was mayhem. The floor appeared to have been transformed into a virtual war zone. The chronics had taken up their posts. They had no time to go to the bathroom. One stood in a puddle.

The wheelies were in their wheel chairs that now doubled as jeeps. They were patrolling the hallways. One jeep flipped over when it hit the puddle next to the sentry. One driver made his own sounds of sirens and guns.

In the meantime, the veggies were hunkering down in their beds – now foxholes. Unfortunately, some of the veggies who had never walked in years were not in their beds. They had found new foxholes in, or under, the beds of others. Presumably, the new foxholes provided better cover. Most of the veggies had their heads down. One sniper raised his arms as if he had a gun. He aimed towards the siren-sounding jeep driver and made a "pop" sound. "Got him," he growled. The next day the audio portion of the alarm system was disconnected.

The Pine Rest building in which I worked.

* * * * *

I began my seminary training in the fall of 1967. The period from the late 1960's through the early 1970's was a period unlike any other. The war in Viet Nam was continuing and was strongly opposed by young people especially on campuses. There were many demonstrations by students opposed to the war. On May 4, 1970 one student on Kent State University was shot to death while participating in an antiwar rally.

As a result of the war, students began to question the authority, not only of government but of everyone. Students and professors often clashed. Debates were frequent and pointed. Professors were challenged as never before.

Occasionally the debates would become personal. In one of my classes a student told the professor that he was a very poor instructor, to which the professor responded "and you are a very poor student."

I had a full course load that consisted of five or six courses at any one time and classes went as scheduled. Most professors were competent and considerate.

One professor became a casualty of the student unrest and left the seminary. His name was P. Y. De Jong. Although he was an excellent preacher, he was a failure as a teacher and his classes were poorly attended. I believe he rectified the problem by imposing a new rule. If anyone skipped more than three classes they would fail. Consequently, his classes were filled with students who were not wholly receptive to his style of teaching. Some deeply resented the need to attend.

When he taught, he would move his chair as close to the students as possible. He would then sit on the back of the chair with his feet on the seat. He seemed incapable of talking with his students. His delivery was the same as when he preached. It was demeaning and the students resented it. One day his lecture was on shepherding. His point was that a pastor is like a shepherd who is vigilant to protect his sheep.

"So what is it that shepherds dooooo?" he intoned as he drew out the last word. No one answered. All were looking downward.

"Well, isn't it obvious, gentlemen? They protect the sheeeep," he intoned again.

One student had enough. Suddenly he was crawling on the floor. "Baa, Baa," he bleated as he crawled between the desks. "Baa," he bleated again as he rubbed his face against the professor's chair. "I've found my shepherd." With that he walked out.

Everyone was shocked, including the professor. Finally he said, "Is there anyone else that has anything to say?"

Everyone was quiet. Then one student spoke. He told how the students hated to be preached at, how demeaning it was and how we resented it. He also talked about the content of the lectures and said they were like Sunday school lessons. Eventually all the students had their say, including me. We gave many examples of the simplistic nature of his lectures. We suggested that the course be dropped. Throughout the ordeal, the professor had been the picture of self-restraint. Finally he said, "Thank you, gentlemen," and left. As it turned out, it was his last lecture.

I was told that a few days after the incident, the professor met with the Board. The meeting had been scheduled well before the classroom blow-up. The purpose of the meeting was to grant the professor permanent tenure. In the meantime, the Board had learned about the incident. They wanted to know more. They suggested that the issue of tenure be postponed until they had time to investigate.

The professor was a proud man. He had been at the seminary for many years and his colleagues respected him. Word was that he would be the next president of the seminary. Certainly he appeared to have the credentials. "It will be now or never," he is alleged to have said. The Board was not moved so the professor left. It was rumored that he walked to the end of the driveway, took off his shoes, shook off the dust, and cursed the seminary. Apparently, the ritual was part of an Old Testament curse.

What is known is that he was profoundly disappointed, some say bitter. He eventually became a pastor for a large church in Sioux Center, Iowa. I understand that he worked tirelessly to establish another seminary in the region. The irony is that the professor's son eventually became the president of Calvin Seminary, the very position the father had always wanted.

On one occasion the student's rebelliousness extended to the churches. During the school-year vacant churches would often call the seminary and ask whether any student was available to preach on a given Sunday. One student accepted the invitation and is alleged to have taken the large pulpit Bible and thrown it on the floor. He then jumped on the Bible and shouted, "is this what you think standing foursquare on the Bible means?" Shortly thereafter the Seminary received a letter stating that that student would never again be permitted to preach in their church. They then described what he had done.

* * * * *

In February of our first year, Delbert was born. The seminary's secretary made a large placard announcing the name, date and weight of each newborn. It was also the custom that the father would provide the coffee for all the seminarians.

One seminarian bought beer when his child was born. The smell caused the professors to become aware of it. The Board of Directors was to meet at the seminary that afternoon. The professors were not impressed. Even though it was cold, they opened all the windows, and ordered that the remaining beer be taken home.

We made new friends. We were particularly close to Rodger and Marge Slater. Joyce and Marge exchanged child-care duties. Both Rodger and I had outside jobs. Occasionally he would come to Pine Rest during my shift and we would study together throughout the night.

After our first year, Joyce and I accepted a summer assignment to pastor a church in Hartley, Iowa. One noon we were having lunch. Del was in his infant seat that was on the table. Neither of us noticed that his feet touched the table. He was slowly pushing himself off. Fortunately, he was tightly strapped into the infant seat. The back of the seat was slightly higher than his head. Consequently, when the seat fell off the table, the back of the seat struck the floor first. Nevertheless, Del cried uncontrollably. We did not realize that his crying was a good sign. We were frantic.

A doctor's office was located directly across the street. We rushed Del to his office. Perhaps the receptionist heard us coming. Despite the fact that the waiting room was full, we were immediately ushered in. We told the doctor what had happened. He examined Del and told us not to worry. Del would be fine. There were no physical injuries, and his crying indicated that he did not have a concussion.

When we returned to Grand Rapids we found

a new suite. It was the main floor of a house located directly across the street from Pine Rest. This enabled me to walk to work. Pine Rest was located on a large tract of land. The building in which I worked, but which no longer exists, was set back from the street, giving the property an estate look. In some places there were trees between the buildings and the street. The grounds were always well kept. Most patients were permitted to walk on the grounds and many did. The mental deficiencies of some patients could be seen simply by the way they looked, walked or talked.

When I went to work, I simply jaywalked across the street. One day, as I was crossing the street, I noticed a police car waiting for a red light. He was facing me. Almost immediately, he turned on his flashing lights. By the time he reached the point where I had crossed, I was on the grounds of the hospital. He said something, but given the noise from the traffic, I could not make it out. He got out of his car and shouted for me to stop but I kept walking. He then ran up behind me and grabbed me by the shoulder. "I told you to stop," he shouted as he turned me around. I had contorted my face. My mouth was open. I started to shake. "Wha... wha... what da...da... da...do you wa... wa... wa... want?" I stuttered. He looked bewildered. "I'm sorry," he said, and left. He thought I was a patient.

In August of 1969, Vincent was born. Because of

his anticipated birth, we did not accept a summer assignment and I continued to work full-time at Pine Rest.

We had no extra money. Our net income was spent on groceries, rent, tuition and car maintenance, including gas. After Del was born, Joyce was no longer able to work outside the home, although she did some babysitting for other seminarians.

In our last Christmas while I was in seminary, we were unable to buy presents for our two little boys. Consequently, both Joyce and I volunteered to give blood. Each of us would receive $20 (enough for their presents) but neither of us was accepted as donors. Joyce was rejected because it was too soon after the birth of Vincent. I was rejected because I had had asthma. Fortunately, our parents sent some gifts.

It was also in my last year that I collapsed. I was at work and suddenly I could barely move. Every movement required an effort. I felt very old. The staff called the doctor. He examined me for a long time and finally concluded that I was suffering from dehydration and exhaustion. The hospital gave me a leave of absence with an invitation to return when I was well. The doctor gave me some medication. Two weeks later I was back at work.

In the spring of 1970 I prepared for final exams. If I passed the written exams, I would be granted my Bachelor of Divinity degree. However, I would still not be eligible to pastor a church. Each seminarian would then be interviewed by a group of professors. I remember the very first question. It was: "Do you think God lives in that light bulb?"

If the professors believed that you were of good character and were competent to pastor a church, they would recommend you to the Synod of the denomination. The Synod would endorse the recommendations and in turn would recommend you to the churches. The pictures of all seminarians recommended by the Synod would appear in "The Banner," which was the official publication of the Christian Reformed Church. At least two of my classmates were not recommended.

Candidates for the ministry

THE BANNER is pleased to present the pictures of the men declared by the Synod of 1970 to be candidates for the ministry in the Christian Reformed Church. See announcement page for addresses and other information.

The announcement in the Banner introducing my graduating class

The vacant churches in need of pastors eagerly scanned the pictures and biographical information. I received two calls from Canada and two from the United States. I visited the two churches in the U.S. and accepted the call to a small church in a small town in Iowa.

In August 1970 we moved our family to Iowa. I drove a U-Haul truck with our few possessions and Joyce followed in our car. She had Vince with her and I had Del with me. There were no seatbelts in the truck. Most of the time Del stood next to me. Occasionally, he would sit on my lap and help me drive. When he slept his head was on my lap. It reminded me of the time I drove home with my father and he had comforted me.

Although Del was only two and a half years old, he had already developed a wonderful sense of curiosity. He wanted to know everything. I told him where we were going and why we were moving. I told him that we had been given a special assignment. It was to let people know that God loved them. From time to time we would sing together.

CHAPTER 4
THE MINISTRY

When we arrived in Iowa, we were eager to get to work. There were only twenty-five families who were members of the church. Joyce and I made a point of visiting most of them as soon as possible. The parishioners were, for the most part, good, honest and hard-working; the kind of people one would expect to find in mid-America. Nonetheless all the names of all the parishioners as well as the names of all the neighboring pastors have been changed for reasons that will become obvious.

The parsonage was an attractive, large two-storey home. The office was located next to the front door. The kitchen was well organized and well equipped, with an adjoining dining room. The living room was large. The upstairs had four spacious bedrooms. The house was perfect for us.

The church itself was almost new. It was a lovely building. Obviously, the parishioners had sacrificed to build it. Apparently, there had been hopes that the church would grow. It was much larger than was necessary to accommodate twenty-five families.

Our church in Iowa

The church did grow. Almost immediately attendance was up. We were finally doing what both of us had worked so hard to attain. We were serving a church. Joyce was particularly happy. She finally had a suitable home for her family and the parishioners loved her. This was also her ministry and she was a gracious host.

On one occasion, a man came to our door. He was a

member of our church and his name was Tom Timmons. Joyce answered the door and led him into the living room where I was reading.

"How are you, Tom?" I asked.

He said nothing. He was trembling.

"What's the matter, Tom?" I asked again.

"Sarah just left me," he burst. That was all he could say. He wept for what seemed like hours. Sarah was his wife. Eventually he began to talk. He often paused to wipe his eyes or nose, or simply to cry. Her leaving was completely unexpected.

He had found a letter from her on their counter. He gave it to me to read. It was only one page. She said she didn't love him anymore. Probably never had. She and John were together now. They had been seeing each other for a long time and were very much in love. She was taking from the house what belonged to her. He could have everything else. She wanted nothing from him. John was all she wanted. It was signed:

"Sorry... Sarah."

I did not know John but Tom did. John was a married man with children. I thought about the carnage left behind.

Tom was not a fighter; he was trying to accept his fate. Occasionally, he would lie face down on the couch and weep into the pillows. Often he would stare vacantly into space. Sometimes he would sleep. His grief was

73

manifest.

He was in no hurry to leave. The afternoon stretched into evening and the evening into night. He did not want to go home. Joyce said he could sleep in the spare bed but he declined. He said he would like to stay where he was. We told him that was okay. The next morning he was still on the couch – asleep.

The next day was Saturday. I had to prepare a sermon for Sunday so Joyce was left to care for Tom. She brought him something to eat and when she sensed that he wanted to talk, she would listen. She gave him time and space to grieve. Late in the afternoon he left to stay with his parents.

Joyce has the gift of empathy. When people confide in her, they feel emotionally safe.

About a month later I saw Tom again. "How are to you, Tom?" I asked.

"Better," he said.

He then told me that he was trying to accept his loss. He said he had spoken with Sarah. She had suggested that he try to sell the house, which he thought he would do. He was sure she would never return.

I could see the tears in his eyes, but he kept his composure. "Thank Joyce for me," he said. "You are so very lucky." I nodded.

* * * * *

Joyce's faith has always been a part of her. She is as certain about what the Bible says as she is about her own existence. She wanted everyone to come to a saving knowledge of Jesus Christ. She did everything she could to make it happen.

She was a woman in love with her husband, her children, her church and with her circumstances. She was fulfilled. She was as happy as I had ever seen her.

In February 1973, our daughter Laura was born. Joyce told me later that she had never felt so complete. She remembered one circumstance in particular. She was shopping and Laura was in a baby carriage. The boys toddled on behind. The ministry was going well and her husband seemed happy. She felt an overwhelming sense of wellbeing. Joyce was particularly happy with me. I had become the pastor she always hoped I would be. Clearly the ministry was successful. I was busy and appeared to be fully engaged in my work.

Soon our church was considered the place to be, especially by young people. The evening service was tailored to young people, and was always well attended. I bought a very large Harley Davidson motorcycle and went everywhere with it. The young people loved it. At first, some of the older parishioners were apprehensive but eventually they came to accept it. Shortly thereafter

75

two neighboring pastors also bought motorcycles.

The family on the Harley

Some of the work was routine. There were "home visitations." These were formal visits of each family, made by the minister and a church elder. The purpose was to assess the spiritual health of the family.

The elder I most enjoyed, and most often went with on home visits, was Alger Braun. He was a retired farmer and hence had time. He was well read and enjoyed the work. He had a quick wit. He was a small man and perhaps that is why he was so funny – he had to be to survive as a child. He always had a joke and loved to make people laugh. When visiting the parishioners, he could be blunt, but never offensive.

Most visits were uneventful. Some were awkward. One was a visit I promised myself never to repeat. We made the visit in December 1970. It was our first winter and very cold. There were two sisters and a brother living together in a small house. All were middle-aged and overweight. None had married. They had been members of the church for many years. The folks were pleasant enough, albeit somewhat simple.

When we arrived in the house, the heat was overwhelming. There was a large wood-burning stove at the side of the kitchen. It had clearly been well fed. The fire crackled happily. Almost immediately we were offered tea. They asked if we used cream. I said "no." Alger said "yes" so a pitcher of cream was put on the table.

Suddenly, it was as if the whole house moved. Cats were coming from everywhere. Most were coming from other rooms, perhaps there to escape the intense heat. There must have been at least a dozen, probably more. Naturally, a catfight started on the table. Some of the cats had colds. Snot was flying everywhere. Cat hair floated on my tea. It took the best efforts of all three occupants to separate the combatants and confine them in two adjoining rooms.

When all the cats were gone, one of the sisters poured what little cream was left into my tea. She must have forgotten that I had said "no." The very last of the cream however, was too thick to pour and she scraped the residue into Alger's cup with a spoon. I did all I could to keep from gagging. They kept urging me to drink my tea. Cookies were placed directly on the table. Some were broken. They asked me if I was okay. I said "yes."

Fortunately, Alger was a gregarious individual. He talked while I looked for a crack in the floorboards to pour the tea. I found none. Eventually, the agony was over and we left, the tea untouched.

As the church grew, the elders took over the responsibility for an increasing number of visits.

Although the folks we had visited were somewhat simple, they meant well and attempted to be helpful. They also changed the way we conducted one evening service.

Generally speaking, evening services were structured to be more casual than the morning services. The intent was to make the services more attractive to young people. To that end, once a month, the evening service would have special music. People could volunteer to participate and many did. Most were family groups, often singing as a mixed quartet or a duet. There was one husband and wife team that sang beautifully and were often called on.

We never turned down those who wished to volunteer. Occasionally I would encourage others to do the same, and on one occasion the two sisters who had served us tea responded.

On a particular Sunday and with the help of their brother they dragged a dilapidated portable keyboard on stage. By the time they were ready to sing they were already out of breath. One of the sisters planted herself behind the keyboard. They were in no hurry. This was likely the first time they were on stage and they seemed determined to make the most of it.

The keyboard which now looked small, was out of tune, but even if it wasn't, it wouldn't have made any difference. The sisters couldn't carry a tune. With obvious enthusiasm one pounded on the keyboard as together they shrieked and howled their way through "Jesus Loves Me" and other simple songs. When finished they were clearly proud of what they had done. They smiled broadly when I thanked them.

Thereafter, I never again called for volunteers. Special music was provided by invitation only.

* * * * *

Early in the ministry, I received a call from Alger. He told me about a religious radio program that he listened to regularly and enjoyed very much. The name of the evangelist was Billy James Hargis. His ministry was located in Tulsa, Oklahoma. In addition to his radio ministry, he was the pastor of a large church and the president of a college that he had started. The college was called the "American Christian College." Hargis was organizing a large convention to be held at the college in a few weeks and he advertised the convention on his radio program.

Alger asked if I wanted to go. I agreed and eventually we left. The experience can best be described as unusual. When we arrived we noticed that many students had revolvers strapped to their thighs. Many also had small American flags stitched onto their shirts. The place looked like a training academy for police officers. We asked one of the students why so many were carrying guns. He said that it was to let everyone know that they were prepared to fight for God and country.

The convention was held in a large auditorium and was well attended but not full. They began by reciting the Pledge of Allegiance and then they sang the National Anthem. The song leader was an energetic and enthusiastic person. Before the National Anthem he had given a short speech, talking about how God had blessed America and particularly Tulsa. He said the least we could do in response to this blessing was to sing the Anthem so loudly that God would hear it. It was clear that for the song leader, there was no distinction between God and country.

He then began a rousing rendition of the Anthem. I was standing at attention, but not singing. Suddenly over the music he began to shout, "stop-stop." The music stopped. It was absolutely quiet. He glared and then pointed at me. "What's the matter with you?" he demanded through clenched teeth, "Isn't this country good enough for you?"

"I'm a Canadian," I shouted back. "If you play the Canadian National Anthem, I will sing it alone." The song leader thought for a moment. "I like that," he said with a smile. He then went on and said he hoped that everyone in that room would be as proud of their country as I obviously was of Canada. Furthermore if any of them were ever in another country they were not to sing that country's National Anthem. "You cannot serve two masters," he concluded.

Alger enjoyed a drink, especially with his evening meal. He soon learned, however, that Tulsa was located in a dry county. This meant that he could not buy a drink at a bar. Instead, he could bring a bottle to the bar and the bartender would mix it for him. We had searched for a liquor store the evening before but had found nothing.

During a break at the convention, I asked one of the student organizers if he knew where we could get some liquor. He said "yes," but he was in a hurry. He told me to meet him at his office after that day's program. He jotted down his address and we agreed to meet at 5:30. I noted that his office was less than two blocks from our hotel. Just before 5:30, I walked to what he had called his office. It was actually a ground floor apartment. I assumed that he lived there.

When I knocked, he opened the door. There was some small talk. I told him that I liked his "office," as he called it. He said he called it his office because that's where he did his best work. I then asked him where I could get some liquor. He said I could have a drink with him. I told him that I didn't drink, but that I wanted to get something for my elder.

He stepped toward the kitchen. I thought he was going to get me something. Then he turned back and looked at me. "Do you swing both ways?" he asked with some hesitation. I had no idea what he was talking about, but I didn't want to look stupid. If I said no, I would probably never know what the other way was. If I said yes than at least I would know. "I swing more ways than you will ever know," I said with certainty.

"Oh, that's good," he said as he dropped his pants and then his underpants. "Let's go." He was standing naked from the waist down. I was shocked. I had not expected this. I wished that I had not said what I did.

"I'm not swinging on that," I murmured as I dashed for the door. I ran back to the hotel and told Alger what had happened. His drink would have to wait.

Several months later Alger told me that Hargis was no longer on the radio. He said that he had called the college and someone told him that Hargis had been accused of inappropriate sexual relations with some of the students, both male and female. I was left to wonder if one of the students was the person I had met.

There was another evangelist in Tulsa at that time. He also had a large church. His name was Oral Roberts. Apparently Roberts and Hargis had a not-so-friendly rivalry.

Oral Roberts also had a radio ministry. I believe it was called "The Abundant Life." In his radio messages he would often stress the healing power of prayer. He said that in his church there was a "Prayer Tower." People who were in physical or mental distress were urged to call his prayer team, and they would pray for the caller. The prayer team was available twenty-four hours a day. There would never be a time when there would not be someone available in the Prayer Tower. Even as he spoke there would be people on their knees, praying on behalf of the callers.

In his radio ministry he would often invite people to come to the Prayer Tower. Given that we were in Tulsa anyway we decided to do so. The Tower was in the middle of the Oral Roberts University complex. It looked like an airport control tower. Next to the elevator was a drop box for contributions. The elevator took us up. We stepped into a rotunda. The view was fantastic but there was no one there. There was only a desk, some chairs and another drop box, nothing else.

We wondered if there might be some sort of a "Prayer machine" where the people's distress calls were recorded, but we could find nothing. We assumed that the prayer team had gone for coffee. We decided to come back later, which we did. There was still no one. After that, his radio messages didn't seem to have the same ring of truth.

*   *   *   *   *

In the spring of 1971, I volunteered to become the director for a summer "Bible Camp." It was a religious retreat for all young people in the region. I knew all the psychiatrists and psychologists from Pine Rest and I invited many of them to attend as counselors. To my pleasant surprise, almost all accepted.

Previous camps had been plagued by bad behavior. Some campers drank openly, and were often drunk. Some used drugs. Some slept all day, and partied all night. The previous year many of the volunteer staff had become discouraged and returned home partway through. Some churches were no longer supporting the camp.

Our camp, however, was a success. It was the

largest camp ever held in the region and there was not a single act of inappropriate behavior. I was there with my motorcycle. Someone suggested that we try to get as many people on the bike as possible. No feet could be touching the ground and we had to travel at least 100 yards – the length of a football field. The number turned out to be twelve.

Many campers received professional and personal help. Others openly and publicly committed their lives to Jesus. Almost all returned home changed; many came back to their churches with a new enthusiasm.

At camp someone had created a "Jesus cheer." It went something like this:

Give me a J –"J," give me an E – "E," give me an S – "S," give me a U – "U," give me an S –"S." Who do we want? "Jesus." Who do we serve? "Jesus."

At a subsequent ministerial meeting one minister complained that a group of campers had interrupted his service with a Jesus cheer. He didn't know it, but it made my day.

An organization called "Youth for Christ" heard of the camp and a delegation was sent to our church. They invited me to be a part of their ministry. They would organize rallies in various towns and cities, and I would be the guest speaker. Unfortunately, I could not accept because I was busy. I did, however, agree to speak at one rally that was being organized in our region. It was scheduled for the following summer. The rally turned out to be a lesson in humility.

It had been organized for a small town. Most small towns in the region were similar. Almost all had an open square in the middle of town and on one corner of the square was a band shell. It was a Sunday afternoon. I arrived on my motorcycle with one of my young people with me.

Near the band shell was a flat bed trailer attached to a large truck. On the trailer was a sound system with enormous speakers. The music could be heard for miles around. It was immediately obvious that the organizers had done a good job. The square was filled with young people listening to the music. The square itself was completely surrounded by cars. They all faced inward, that is, towards the square.

When the time came, I was introduced. I no longer remember the message, but it would have been a message of hope. After the message there was a short prayer, and then an altar call. During the altar call the music played softly. The song was "Just as I Am."

The response was almost immediate. Many responded to the invitation to accept Jesus as their personal Savior. Some were very emotional. The counselors directed the respondents to a quieter area behind the speakers where they could speak and pray with them. I was told that over fifty young people had responded.

After what seemed like a long time the chief organizer came to me. I thought he was going to thank me and inform me that the meeting was over. From their point of view it had been an obvious success.

Instead he said, "The counselors tell me that there are a number of young people who are undecided. They believe that if you tell them again that now is the time to decide, they will respond positively. Let them know that Jesus is calling and that this is their chance to respond. Who knows, it may be their only chance."

I was reluctant. "What do we have to lose?" he said. "If they do not respond, they are in no worse position than now. But if they do respond, praise God. Further, this may also be our last chance to speak to them." I agreed. I climbed back onto the flatbed and I repeated the altar call. The music was turned up slightly but the mood had changed. Some in the crowd had already returned to their vehicles. The most enthusiastic listeners had already responded and were behind the speakers.

Approximately half way through the second call someone in a vehicle on the left hand side of the square blew their horn. Someone from the right responded, then the left, then the right. Each time, more cars joined in. It was like an audio ping-pong game. Then from the far side a trucker blasted his air horn. Perhaps he wanted the others to stop. But they did not. The game was not over.

87

There was no way I could continue. The organizers turned up the music. I left the flatbed; quickly put on my helmet, pulled it down as low as possible, and started the Harley. My passenger jumped on without a word and we left as quietly as possible. The problem is that it is difficult to quiet a Harley. I was surprised when I was invited back.

* * * * *

I am not sure why, but young people in particular seemed to respond to our ministry. One such person was Matt. He was a good-looking university student and I liked him. We had spoken on several occasions. On one occasion he gave us the records of the musical "Jesus Christ Superstar." I promised to listen.

Not long thereafter, he called. He asked if we had listened to the records. I said "yes." He asked if he could come over to talk about it. I said "yes." We talked throughout the evening. Joyce often joined us. He said that he had been involved in the occult. He was not a Christian. In fact, he said he could not physically hold a Bible. When he did, it made him sick. He had however listened to "Jesus Christ Superstar" and had also heard me speak.

He had many questions. He was not happy with his current lifestyle. He was looking for a new direction. His parents were genuine Christians. It was clear that he was ready to make the same commitment his parents had made. By the end of the evening, he had committed his life to Jesus.

Not everyone responded as Matt had. There was Dr. Marshall who was a physician. His wife and daughter attended our church. She asked me if I would talk to her husband. I said "yes." We set up a time near Christmas.

When we arrived he was inhospitable and direct. "What do you want?" he asked.

"Your wife asked me to see you," I answered.

"Oh, yes," he said. "She's been telling me all about your preaching. Do you really believe that stuff?"

"Like what?" I asked.

"Like Mary being impregnated by God."

"Yes," I said.

"Do you have any proof?' he asked (knowing that proof was impossible).

"No," I said, "the Holy Spirit assures me that what I say is true."

He looked at me in disbelief. "You believe that what you're saying is true because a spirit told you so?"

"Also, because the Bible says so," I said.

"Did that spirit also tell you that what the Bible says is true?"

I did not answer.

"That's a pretty busy spirit," he said, "no wonder

they call it the Holy Ghost."

He then invited me to leave. "You're probably good at what you do," he said, "but I'm not buying any ghost stories."

Our talk had lasted less than five minutes.

* * * * *

Not every call was of a spiritual nature. One night at about 11:30, I received a call from a lady. She sounded anxious. She asked me if I could come over. She said she had something important to discuss, but not on the phone. "Please," she pleaded.

I agreed. She had been living with her boyfriend on an acreage outside of town. Both were in their mid-thirties. They had been coming to our church on a regular basis. I had spoken with them many times.

When they first came to church, he was on parole. The condition of his parole was that he not drink. Apparently, when he was drunk, he was a violent, obnoxious, unpredictable individual. However, when sober, he was one of the most likeable people I have ever met. He looked like Robert Redford. Unfortunately, he violated the condition of his parole. At the time of the phone call, he was in jail.

After the phone call, I called Andy, my deacon. He was the father of Matt. I told him about the phone call.

90

He readily agreed to accompany me as I knew he would. We drove to the acreage and knocked on the door. She opened the door wide and warmly invited me in. She did not immediately see Andy. She was wearing nothing but a see-through negligee and no underwear. When she saw Andy she was shocked; but not as shocked as Andy. He stood there with his mouth open. He had expected a deep spiritual conversation. He had his Bible in his hand.

She recovered quickly. "Oh, I'm sorry," she said. "I was not expecting you so soon." I asked her if she preferred that we talk another day. She said "yes" and we left. I visited the boyfriend in jail a couple of times, but they never came back to church. I assume she felt embarrassed.

* * * * *

I do not remember all the parishioners. There are some however, that I remember well. There was a sports bar in town that served very good food. I often went there, either by myself or with others. I eventually became friends with the owner whose nickname was Duke. Most people knew him by that name only.

Even though he was not a Christian, he seemed very interested in what I believed and asked many questions. Over time he and his entire family attended church on a regular basis. He was not an emotional or demonstrative person but he quietly became a Christian.

Every spring he would drive to Brownsville, Texas in a refrigerated van. The purpose of the trip was to obtain fresh produce for his bar. On one occasion I went with him. Brownsville is on the border with Mexico. Duke wanted only fresh vegetables. Arrangements had been made with a local farmer to obtain the veggies directly from the farm. Mexicans tended the fields and, clearly, most of the workers were in the country illegally. When we drove into the field with the van, they fled. Someone blew a loud whistle and they returned. That was their signal.

There is nothing like a road trip to get to know someone. Hours on the road give ample opportunity to talk. He asked me about the ministry, my background and my faith. I asked him about bartending and his background. I learned that no one knows the townspeople better than a bartender. He had heard many confessions. Lips are loosened by liquor. News spreads quickly. People talk. In fact, he had heard about me shortly after I arrived. People were talking about this new Harley-riding pastor in town. One person had heard me preach. "He said that you sounded like Billy Graham, and that I should hear you."

"Who said that?" I asked.

"Tom Timmons," he answered.

Tom was the person whom Joyce had comforted.

I asked him why people called him Duke.

He said that sometimes when people drank too much they would forget his name. So they just called him Duke.

I asked him what he would like to pass on to his children.

"I would like them to be Christian" he said, then added with chuckle "and I hope they never drink."

*   *   *   *   *

Another person I remember well was a young lady, probably in her late twenties. She and her husband lived in a rented farmhouse. They had no children and both worked full time. She had a reputation for being easy. Nevertheless, she was always willing to help. She had a wonderful sense of humor and she laughed easily. She came from a conservative Christian home.

She was not a beautiful woman and wouldn't have made it in Hollywood but she was attractive. Like the Mona Lisa, she had an allure. Her name was Cathy Short.

One day I was notified that she was in the hospital and I went to visit her. On duty was a nurse I knew. She was not a member of our church, but, along with her family, she attended regularly. When I arrived, I told the nurse that I was there to see Cathy. We engaged in some small talk. Then she said, "Pastor, I think there is

93

something you should know. The doctors can't find anything wrong with her."

"Why is she here then?" I asked.

"Because she can't walk," she answered. "She seems paralyzed. The doctors think it's psychological."

I thanked her and went to see Cathy. We talked for about a half hour, but it was idle chit-chat. I tried to get her to open up but she had resisted.

Finally I said, "Cathy, if we were Catholic, and you were in a confessional, what would you say to God?"

She thought for a long time. She was absolutely still – except for the expression on her face. I said nothing. Then she began to weep uncontrollably. She put a pillow over her face so as to muffle the sound. She wept without restraint; long, deep anguished sobs. I waited. "I'm such a slut," she whispered. Again she wept. I took her hand.

"Would you like to talk about it?" I asked.

"No," she said. But she did anyway. "I can't seem to say no; I can't control myself." she sobbed. "I'm such a slut," she repeated. Between each whispered sentence she cried.

Nevertheless, the dam had broken. Through tears she began to open up. She talked about her husband and what a good person he was, how lucky she was to have him and how she had hurt him. He had found her with another man. He had forgiven her but he didn't know the half of it, she said. There had been many. Sometimes her words were nothing more than a whimper. "I'm such a slut," she concluded.

She said she had prayed for strength but had done it anyway. "God hates me," she said. "I feel so guilty." Eventually she stopped crying. She lay in her bed looking blankly at the ceiling.

Now it was my turn to talk. I remembered what the nurse had said: "The doctors think it's psychological." Was it possible that Cathy was paralyzed by guilt, self-incrimination and remorse?

"Cathy," I said, "I want to tell you something, but before I do please promise to hear me out." She nodded but said nothing.

"Do you think God could forgive a murderer?" I asked. She nodded.

"What if he killed his own child?" She nodded again.

"What if he killed his own wife?" She nodded.

"What if he tortured his wife before he killed her?"

"God could, "she said, "if he became a Christian."

"Cathy," I said abruptly, "God forgave you before this conversation even started. You believe that God could forgive a murderer because Jesus died for him, but your sins are too big for God to forgive. Do you really think that God would prefer to punish you rather than accept the gift that Jesus made on your behalf?"

"In the grand scheme of things, your sins are not

that big, Cathy. In fact, if that's all there was, Jesus would not have had to die; a good beating would have been sufficient."

She looked at me and began to laugh.

"You take yourself too seriously," I said. "You paralyzed yourself with guilt and remorse and for what? For sins already paid for?"

"We both know you did wrong, and we both know you want to fix it. It shouldn't be that difficult. What you need is a psychiatrist—not punishment. There's nothing wrong with you that a little counseling can't fix."

I took her by the hand. "Let's go, Cathy," I said. "I'll take you home."

She stepped out of bed and took a few steps, then stopped. "I'm walking," she whispered in disbelief. I nodded.

"I'm walking," she shouted, "I'm walking." She threw her arms around my neck and hugged me. Then she ran down the hallway to the nurses' station. The back of her gown was open, but it didn't matter. "I'm walking," she shouted through tears. She hugged all the nurses in turn. She couldn't stand still. She kept jumping up and down. "I don't know what happened," she said, "but I'm okay now. I'd like to go home."

"You can't go home," the nurse answered, "until the doctor sees you."

That afternoon she was discharged.

She later told me she was seeing a counselor. She said she was stronger now. With a wink she said that her husband was happy. "Thank you, Winson," she said.

After I left the ministry, I received a number of letters from Leroy Terpstra (a neighboring pastor). I had seldom responded. We had already been living in Edmonton for a number of years when Leroy phoned. The purpose of the call was to inquire why I so rarely responded to his letters. I told him I had been busy but that I would write in the future. After some further small talk, he said:

"Winson, do you remember Cathy Short?"

"Yes, I do," I replied.

"And do you remember Aaron Tubis?" he continued.

"Yes," I said. (Aaron had been a member of our church). "Why?"

"They had an affair. Somehow it got out. His wife left with the kids for a while, but I think she's back now. Apparently Cathy has been screwing everybody. I screwed her too," he said casually.

"You what?" I stammered.

"Ya," he said, "I screwed her too. Went there to visit and before I knew it we were in the sack. It only happened once though."

I was sick. We talked some more but I only wanted to hang up.

I thought about Cathy a lot that day – the alluring, attractive, fun-loving lady. I thought about how she had prayed for strength and how happy she had been. I wanted to pray for her but I cried instead. Thereafter I received three or four more letters from Leroy, but I never responded.

* * * * *

In the spring of our second year, Joyce planted a garden in the back corner of our lot. One of our neighbors had planted their garden adjacent to ours. One late summer evening I was helping Joyce in the garden and our neighbors were attending to theirs. Occasionally we would engage in casual conversation. Most of the vegetables were fully grown, such that the ground was hardly visible. I may have been picking beans. Suddenly a cat jumped out of the foliage, landed on my shoulder and bit me in the neck. I swiped the cat away and it ran off.

My neighbor saw what happened. "You're bleeding," he said. He came over and looked at my neck. "The cat bit you," he exclaimed. "You have to get it."

"Why?" I asked.

"Because it may have rabies."

He could see I was skeptical. I knew nothing about rabies. I had never known a person who had rabies, and I had never lived in an area where it was a problem.

"You have to get it," he said again. He then went on to tell me about rabies. He said the cat had acted in a peculiar way. Cats don't ordinarily jump onto people and bite them – unless of course they have rabies. If we did not find the cat I would require five injections, all in the stomach and all very painful. The only way to avoid these injections was to capture the cat and prove that it did not have rabies. If it were diseased, I would require the shots anyway.

By this time both Joyce and I were fully alarmed. We set off to find the cat. In the meantime my neighbor ran back to his house and called the sheriff. Soon other neighbors joined in the search. How they found out so quickly, I do not know. Some passers-by asked what was going on. When told, they also joined the search. By the time the sheriff came, we had found the cat. The search party had grown to about twenty people.

The cat was found in the boarded up back yard of a cantankerous old bachelor named George. He lived with his sister but most people had not seen her for years. Many thought she had died. The yard itself had been boarded up with slabs, presumably to hide the junk behind it. The slabs were not uniform so the fence had many holes. It was about five feet high.

The sheriff came out of his car with a .22 caliber rifle. He took aim at the cat using the fence to steady himself. I was standing next to him. Just as he was about to shoot, the owner burst out of his house. He also had a rifle and it was much larger than the sheriff's.

"What the hell are you doing?" he screamed. "You can't shoot that cat. It's my cat and it's on my property. If you shoot that cat, you f...ing son of a bitch, it will be the last f...ing breath you'll ever take." He then pointed his gun at the sheriff.

Soon his sister joined him. I have never seen a person so white. Clearly she had never been exposed to the sun. She looked as though she had just walked out of a flour factory. She was also screaming when she came to the door. "That's my cat, that's my cat." She stepped out as if she intended to retrieve it.

"Stop," the sheriff demanded. He propped his loaded gun against the fence. He then walked along the fence and found a gate next to the house.

"Put the gun down, George," he said. "We need the cat. It may have rabies." He then explained what happened and why we needed the cat. He also told George that if he did not put the gun down, he would have to arrest him. Slowly George turned and retreated into the house, taking his rifle with him. His sister followed.

The sheriff walked back and again took aim at the cat. "I'll never hit that damn thing," he said. "I'm shaking like a leaf."

"I'll shoot it," I said. "I was born on a farm. I've always had a "22" and I'm an excellent shot."

He considered it. "You have to shoot it through the heart," he said. "The brain goes to the lab so it has to remain intact." He then gave me the gun.

Throughout the entire ordeal the cat had remained in the same place. It was partially hidden in a large pile of loose rubble.

I shot. The cat elevated out of the rubble about as high as the fence. Then it fell back onto a plank. It shook momentarily. Then nothing. It was clearly dead. I gave the gun back to the sheriff. Again he walked along the fence and entered the yard through the gate. This time however, he had his gun. He carefully walked through the rubble and picked up the dead cat.

As the incident unfolded the number of spectators increased. I was later told that when the sheriff took hold of the cat, the spectators clapped but I did not hear it. He put the cat into the trunk of his car. We spoke briefly and he said he would contact me as soon as he heard from the lab.

I told him that what he had done was gutsy. "Ah, not really," he said. "I know George. I was surprised when the son of a bitch pointed the gun at me though."

The next afternoon I received a call from him. The cat did not have rabies. Soon everyone in town knew what had happened. Some parishioners jokingly referred to me as the cat killer. Occasionally, people would point me out to their friends. I could see them whisper that I was the pastor who shot the cat with the sheriff's gun.

Unfortunately George was not done. He owned a small parcel of land near the outskirts of town and our home was between George's house and his land. The next day, about mid-morning, George drove by our house on his tractor. Across his lap was his rifle, pointed towards our house. Joyce was the first to see it. That afternoon when the sheriff called with the lab results, I told him about George and the rifle.

"I will talk to him," he said. "If he ever does that again, let me know."

Thereafter, George passed our home many times, but we never again saw the rifle.

One of my friends was a pastor in a neighboring church. His name was Jason Van Horne. Shortly after the event, we met at our place. Jason was not as enthusiastic about the ministry as I was, but he was idealistic. He believed that the Holy Spirit could change lives. I told him about the cat and George. I told him how angry George had been, and that it had been necessary for me to shoot the cat. I also told him that George had driven by with his rifle.

"You know what George needs?" he said when I finished. "He needs to know that Jesus loves him and died for him."

I agreed. I looked out the window and noticed that George was working in his field with his tractor. "He's there now," I said pointing out the window.

"Then let's talk to him," said Jason, and off we went onto his field. We stood where he would be forced to stop.

"What do you want, you bastard?" he shouted.

We approached him, one on each side of his tractor. He had not throttled down so we were forced to speak loudly.

"We want you to know that God loves you, and sent Jesus into this world to die for you," Jason shouted. George looked stunned. I'm not sure what he expected, but this was not it.

"You shot my cat, you f...ing asshole," he screamed, looking at me. He stood up on the tractor. "Get out of here. If I ever see you again I'll blow your f...ing head off. Go!" he yelled.

The Bible says there is a time for everything. This was not the time for evangelizing. I looked at Jason and shrugged my shoulders. It was time to go.

* * * * *

There are a number of Christian Reformed churches in Iowa. At that time most were conservative. There was a prevailing sentiment among many conservatives that Calvin Seminary was a "hot bed" of liberalism. This sentiment was nourished by a number of conservative ministers. They felt the seminary had become so liberal that it was necessary to start their own.

A group of these ministers had organized a meeting to promote the new seminary. This group included: P. Y. De Jong (a former professor at Calvin Seminary who had left in disgrace); John Vander Ploeg (editor-in-chief and managing editor of The Banner); and John Piersma (the former pastor of the First Christian Reformed Church in Pella, Iowa). There were others in the group but these were the major players.

The meeting was to be held in the first Christian Reformed Church in Pella because it was the largest church in the region. All "concerned" Christians were invited to attend. I believe it was held in the winter of 1971 – 72. Although I did not receive a separate invitation, I did eventually learn of the meeting. I was a "concerned" Christian and so was Adam Hynd, my neighboring pastor. We both decided to go.

Fortunately, we arrived early. Although the church was already full, we found two seats near the front. By the time the meeting started, there were people everywhere. The pews were crowded. People were standing along the outside walls and in the back entry. Large speakers transmitted the message into the basement, which was apparently full. The organizers could not have been happier.

The speaker was John Vander Ploeg. I believe that

the moderator was John Piersma. P. Y. De Jong was also on stage and appeared to be acting as a consultant.

The speech was completely negative and designed to inspire those already converted. In essence he said that there were those in Calvin Seminary who no longer believed in:

1. A real 6 day creation,

2. A real historical Adam and Eve,

3. A real serpent and a real paradise, and

4. A real judgment and a real hell with real consequences.

He claimed that there were those in seminary who no longer accepted the first principle of sound biblical interpretation, which is that every word of Scripture is the inspired and inerrant Word of God, not only in matters of faith but also in historical, geographical, and other secular matters.

He alleged that there were those in seminary who restricted the Word of God only to matters of faith. It is at this point that conservatives and liberals come to the crossroads and a parting of the ways, he thundered.

If we cannot believe every word then who decides what is to be believed. If the reality of Adam or the serpent as real historical entities is called into question, then the truth of the reality of Christ must also be questioned. These two stand or fall together. The rejection of any one part, however small, eventually leads to the loss of all.

The second principle of interpretation (no longer accepted by some seminary professors) is that Scripture must be interpreted by Scripture. In other words, the Bible is true because the Bible says so. He denounced the emerging pattern of thinking that looked at Scripture in the light of reason or laboratory findings.

After the speech the moderator spoke in a loud baritone voice. "Wasn't that wonderful?" he boomed. "We are so blessed that there are still some who are prepared to tell us the truth about Calvin Seminary. But we can make it right. We can start our own seminary. It will be based on true principles of interpretation."

"Our offering will be for the new seminary. I know you will give generously. There is an obvious need."

"There will also be an opportunity to ask questions. It would be a shame not to hear more. Therefore, if you have any questions, please write them down and put them into the collection plate, along with your generous gifts. We will do our best to answer all your questions."

While the organ played I had scribbled down some questions. Mostly, I wanted to know whom he was talking about. During the speech I had whispered to

Adam, "Do you know who he's referring to?"

"No," he answered.

I believe P. Y. De Jong had taught the Principles of Scriptural Interpretation while at the seminary a few years previously. If he had not actually taught the course he certainly would have applied the principles to whatever course he was teaching.

There was something wrong with this picture. The speaker was condemning the seminary from which P. Y. De Jong had sought permanent tenure. And P. Y. was supporting him. Perhaps the previous professor had some insider information, and I wanted to know what it was.

After the "generous" contributions and questions were gathered, the moderator started again. He read the questions and the speaker answered. It was apparent, at least to us, that this was a charade. The questions simply enabled the speaker to repeat what he had said.

"Has he answered any of your questions yet?" I whispered to Adam.

"No," he said.

I had heard enough. I walked up to the pulpit and spoke into the microphone. "I'm a recent graduate of Calvin Seminary which you have denounced. May I have five minutes for a rebuttal?" I looked back at the moderator. He hastily walked back to P. Y. De Jong and the other organizers. They briefly conferred.

Then he came back. "No son," he said. "You cannot. You are no different than anyone else. If everyone wished to speak we would be here all night. You had the opportunity to write whatever questions you might have."

He put his arm around my shoulder and gently pushed me off the stage.

I said nothing, but I did not return to my seat. Rather, I started walking down the middle aisle toward the rear of the church.

Then something remarkable happened. Someone called out "Let the young man speak." There was no answer. Then another called out even more loudly, "Let the young man speak." Then another and another, and then it became a cadence. "Let the young man speak," shouted many in unison.

Finally the moderator regained control. By that time I was standing in the rear of the church. "People, people," he shouted. "Let's have some order. This young man cannot be treated any differently than anyone else. If we let him speak, we must allow everyone to do the same. Now to continue..." and I heard him read the next question.

Some of the people had also heard enough. What had happened had violated their sense of fairness. The seminary had been condemned and they were denied the opportunity to hear the other side.

As I left the church a number of people followed – at first, a few, then more. Soon there was a crowd outside which continued to grow. Someone hoisted me onto the back of a pick-up truck. Then the questions started, and continued into the night.

A loud angry voice sounded from the rear of the crowd. "What do you think of women in office?" he shouted. This was one of those "crossroad" issues that Vander Ploeg had sermonized on. It was a litmus test, which would reveal whether I was a conservative or liberal; whether I was with them or against them.

I knew from the tone of his voice that my answer would alienate him. "I promise I will answer your question," I said, "but before I do, please let me tell you what I really believe." I then recited the Apostles' Creed.

**I believe in God the Father, Almighty, Maker
of heaven and earth.
And in Jesus Christ, His only begotten Son,
our Lord;
Who was conceived by the Holy Spirit, born
of the Virgin Mary;
Suffered under Pontius Pilate; was cruci-
fied, dead, and buried;
He descended into hell;
The third day He rose again from the dead;
He ascended into heaven, and sitteth at the
right hand of God the Father Almighty;**

109

From thence He shall come to judge the living and the dead.
I believe in the Holy Spirit.
I believe in a holy, catholic Church, the communion of saints;
The forgiveness of sins;
The resurrection of the body;
And life everlasting.

"Do you believe what I just recited?" I asked.

"Yes," he answered.

I continued. "Then whatever the answer I give to your question – would that be enough to separate us?"

He thought for a moment. "No," he said.

I then gave him my answer. At that time I believed that women could be ordained as deacons.

The new Mid-America Reformed Seminary which the meeting in the Pella church was meant to spawn, was not born until 1981. P. Y. De Jong was one of their first instructors. Even now, I believe that what happened in the Pella church that night set back the birth of the new seminary for almost a decade.

CHAPTER 5

DISAPPOINTMENTS

Throughout the ministry there were also disappointments, some profound and some less so. None were pleasant.

The Van Winkles

As previously indicated, one of my parish friends was the bar owner. Even though I was often at the bar, I never had a drink. Nevertheless, some of the parishioners found it hard to accept. The only recurring complaint that the church council ever received about me was that I went to the bar. The complaints persisted even though the bar owner and his entire family attended our church regularly. I was fortunate that I had a very supportive council. They generally dealt with the complaints.

One such complaining couple was Morris and Elizabeth (Liz) Van Winkle. They were an older couple, likely in their mid-sixties. They had been life–long members of the church. I'm not sure whether they ever had children. I think not. I do know that they had never driven on a freeway even though there was access to one only a few miles away.

When it was time for their house visitation, I attended with Alger, my favorite elder. We knocked on the door. Morris answered and (without saying anything) went directly to a chair in the corner of the room. The chair was facing the corner, so that Morris's back was to us. We looked around the room and saw Liz sitting the same way in another corner. About the time we walked in, Liz began to wail loudly. Soon Morris was sniffling.

"What's the matter?" we asked almost simultane-ously. There was no answer – except that the wailing became even louder. Morris was making strange guttural sounds when not sniffling. We were both concerned. I thought someone may have died. Despite our persistent inquiries, there was no answer.

Finally, Morris began to talk through the sniffles. "We are not happy with the pastor," he whimpered. He had said it as if I wasn't even there.

Alger and I looked at each other quizzically.

"Why not?" Alger stammered.

"Because....because he goes to the bar," he said in a whisper.

"That's right," wailed Liz, doing her best to conjure up some tears.

Alger began to laugh, 'Are you kidding?" he said. "You rearranged your furniture for that?"

"That's not all," Morris moaned.

"No," wailed Liz even more loudly. "That's not all."

"What else?" Alger asked skeptically.

I said nothing.

Once again the parties went through the same tug of war. Alger would press for answers; Morris and Liz resisted.

Finally Alger suggested that we leave. It was enough to end the stalemate.

"We think...we think," began Morris, wedging the words between sniffles and pauses.

He began again, "we think...." he paused this time to blow his nose.

Liz continued to wail.

"We think..." said Morris slowly and in a faltering voice. "We think that he's a communist."

"Yes," Liz shrieked angrily. "He's a communist."

Back then the cold war was alive and well. There

was no greater insult than to call someone "a communist."

I continued to say nothing. After all, what would a communist have to offer?

Alger did all the talking.

It is not disappointing that a pastor must deal with parochial halfwits, living in a small world of their own making. What was disappointing was that their Christianity had never grown to the point where it could include a bar owner and his family.

Bill Sterbin

The facts below are of such a nature that I have changed all the names. The purpose is to protect the identity of "Gloria." If the circumstances described are similar to the circumstances of people not involved, than such description is purely accidental.

One evening a lady rang the doorbell. I answered. She looked around as if she were afraid that someone would see her. She quickly entered when given the invitation. I had seen her before. Her name was Gloria. She was not a member of our church, but had attended recently. She had a pleasant face with a muscular body. On first sight, she would be the first person chosen if getting work done was the only criterion.

After some pleasantries she said, "I want to talk to you about something, but before I do, I need to know that you will never talk to Bill Sterbin about it."

I was surprised. Bill and his wife Fran were members of our church, albeit she often came alone. I did not know either of them well. However, I did know that at a previous house visitation they had complained about my bar attendance. Two elders had done that visitation. I told Gloria that I would not talk to Bill about what she told me. It was a promise I kept, but came to regret.

She then told me what happened. She had been married to Bill's nephew, Gary. Bill owned a business as well as some property consisting of several parcels of land. One parcel had a lovely home and some out-buildings. She and Gary had lived there since they were married. They had two boys and the oldest was now in kindergarten. The place was ideal for them and although the rent was high it was a wonderful place to raise their boys.

Gary was not much of a father. Bill on the other hand spent countless hours with the boys. He did everything a father would do and showed them how to do things in his shop. When Bill was on his tractor, he would take one of the boys with him. When not working, he would play with the boys or take them fishing. She and Gary had referred to him as Billy the Kid. The boys referred to him as their "other Grandpa."

Unfortunately, things were not good between Gloria and Gary. Eventually they divorced. She did not say why. After the divorce Gary moved to Chicago. He wanted nothing to do with his family. As for the children, nothing much had changed. They loved their other grandpa. When Gary left, Bill told Gloria that she could continue to live in the home rent free.

But Bill was not just interested in the children. After the boys were put to bed he would come on to her. She resisted but he persisted. She kept the boys up as long as possible, but he would outlast them. Eventually Bill gave her an ultimatum. If she did not have sex with him, she would have to pay twice the rent that they had paid before. She did look around for another place, but there was really nothing. There were a few small apartments in a town some twenty miles away. If they moved, she would have to find another kindergarten.

However, even if there had been something suitable, she couldn't afford it anyway. She was living rent-free now. She was working part-time as a receptionist but the income would not be enough. Worse still, if she moved, the boys would no longer have their other grandpa; at least, not on a daily basis. They loved him and they would be devastated. What would she tell them?

Eventually, she relented. Bill was over all the time

and she became pregnant. Both wanted an abortion –
especially Bill. He asked her about it nearly every day.

Through her doctor, she learned of a clinic in New
York. Because abortions were illegal at that time no one
in Iowa would do it.

It had taken some time to make arrangements. By
the time she went to New York, she was nearly three
months along. Bill paid for the trip and for the abortion. He had insisted that she call him after the abortion,
which she did from her hotel room.

When she came to see me she had been home for
about six weeks. Bill was after her again. She knew that
she would have to do something different this time. She
said that she felt guilty and ashamed. She did not know
what she was going to do, except that she would not have
sex with Bill.

We talked for some time.

"If money was no object," I said, "What would you
prefer to do?"

"That's hard to say," she said, "For my sake, I would
like to leave, but for the boys' sake I would like to stay."

"If it wasn't for the sex?" I asked, "Would you stay?"

"Yes," she said.

"Do you have any proof that you had an abortion,
and that Bill paid for it?" I asked.

"I have the boarding passes and a letter from the
clinic confirming the appointment as well as some hotel

receipts," she answered.

I suggested that she use them. She could see where this was going. She began to smile. There was no need to say anything more. We never did speak again. I heard that for a short time she had gone to Chicago but I do not know why. When she returned she continued to live where she always had.

Bill was probably one of the most unattractive men I had ever met. What made him unattractive were his teeth – or should I say "his tooth." He had only one tooth at the upper front and it was partially decayed. He sucked on it constantly – even while talking. I knew that I could not talk to Bill about what Gloria had said, but I wanted to get to know him better. I tried to set up a time to see him but he was always busy. I sought him out after church, but he was always dismissive. It was clear that talking to me was not a high priority for him.

When the next schedule for house visitation was drawn up I told council I wanted to visit him. I asked Alger Braun to accompany me; he agreed. Alger knew Bill well. They had gone to the same church for years.

He said that Bill had changed over the years. When he was young he was a very good baseball player. After he married Fran, he became the president of the "Men's Society," which was a Bible study for men. He had also been on council, first as a deacon, then as an elder. Over time Bill's business had become more and more important to him. Now it was the only important thing in his life.

Alger thought that Bill may have been physically abusive to Fran. I asked him what made him think so. He said Fran would often come to church with bruises on her arms and face. When asked what happened, she would always have an excuse.

I did not tell him that Gloria had seen me, or anything about what she said. However, I did ask him if he would take the lead during the visit. He agreed.

During the visit, Alger did his best. Bill and his wife sat like statues. Neither was forthcoming. Their answers were always one or two words. Even small talk was abrupt.

"Well, Bill, I see that business is good," said Alger cheerfully.

"Not bad."

"The prices are good aren't they?"

"Not bad."

Alger then tried a different approach.

"Have you heard from your nephew Gary?"

"Nope."

"He's in Chicago isn't he?"

'Yep."

"Does he intend to come back?"

"Don't know."

It was time to move on. Alger tried again.

"I see Fran coming to church alone. Is everything okay?"

"Yep."

"You're not sick are you?"

"Nope."

"You weren't there Sunday. Why not?"

"Busy."

I could see the exasperation on Alger's face.

"Do you have any problems with the church or the pastor?" The question seemed to spark some interest.

"Yep," he answered.

"Well what?"

"We don't like that he goes to the bar."

"Bill," Alger said earnestly, "we talked about that last time." He then went on to say that Duke (the bartender) and his family were coming to church and that I had never ordered a drink. In fact, he (Alger) had been there with me.

"Well we still don't like it that he goes," said Bill pointing at me.

"Anything else?"

"Yep," Bill responded, sucking enthusiastically on his tooth.

For the first time he looked at me. "Do you remember that sermon you had on the Song of Solomon? You don't think you can teach us old dogs any new tricks do you?"

He then began to laugh. But it was not a laugh of merriment. It was a fierce laugh motivated by anger. Then, so as to reinforce the point, he began to slap his knee. Abruptly he stopped. "I never want to hear it again," he warned, pointing his finger at me.

I said nothing. It wasn't necessary. Bill's rage was propelling him.

"And why aren't you using the King James Version?" he asked fiercely. "You know don't you? I know you know."

I told him that I thought the version we were using was more understandable.

"You're lying," he said angrily. "I know you're lying."

Alger tried to stop him but there was no stopping him now. He was sucking furiously on his tooth.

"You use the new version because it doesn't mention the blood of Jesus." He then went on a tirade about how many more times the King James Version mentions blood compared to the new version.

"There was a time when preachers weren't afraid to tell the truth. Why don't you preach on hell?" he demanded. He said he could still remember some "real" ministers. And so it went.

"It's no wonder the church is going to hell," he fumed. With that he stormed out.

On the way back Alger asked me if I wanted council

to do anything about Bill. "He called you a liar," he said. "I think council should do something."

"No," I said, "I want to think about it."

The real wrong was not that he called me a liar. The real wrong was what he had done to his niece. The visit was for me a mixture of emotions. They ranged from disbelief, astonishment, anger and revulsion. Here was a man (who had impregnated his niece and financed an illegal abortion) talking about the blood of Jesus. The contrast could not have been greater. I also wanted to knock out that revolting tooth. It would stop that disgusting sucking sound.

On the way home I thought about Gloria and the boys. I knew she was still living there. I don't know what Gloria said or did but I have a theory. I believe that Gloria told Bill about our visit and that is why he was so angry with me. I also believe that Bill did give her another ultimatum and that Gloria told him that if he forced her to leave, she would disclose what he had done. I hope so.

Wilbert

Not all disappointments were in respect to members of our church. Some related to others. One evening Loren knocked on our door. He was about fifteen years old and a member of our church. I taught him catechism. In class he said very little. He was shy and walked with his head down. He was part of the nerd crowd.

I invited him in. He had a hard time expressing himself. Often he hesitated as he searched for words. For most of the conversation he looked at the floor. I kept assuring him that we had time – that what he had to say was important.

Despite his bashfulness, he wasted little time getting to the point. He said there was a fellow in town by the name of Wilbert. His home was a hangout for young people. He lived alone and had all sorts of "sex stuff." He was always trying to have sex with the boys. Loren said that he had been talking to some of his friends. They had decided that they should tell someone. That was why he had come to me.

I thanked him. I told him that I thought he was courageous. I asked him why they had not called the police? He said that one of his friends had a problem with the police. Anyway, they didn't want anyone to know that they had been there – especially their parents. They were also afraid of what Wilbert might do. Loren had told his friends that I would know what to do.

The next day I called the sheriff. (He was the sheriff who had given me his gun to shoot the cat.) Without mentioning any names, I told him what Loren had told me.

"Who told you this?" he asked.

"I can't tell you," I answered.

"I don't suppose he'll give me a signed statement."

"No," I said.

"I can't get a search warrant much less an arrest without something."

"What if he gave you a statement without signing it?" I asked.

"That wouldn't help much," he said. "But why don't we do this: ask him if he will give you a statement. He doesn't have to sign it, but he does have to number it. Then on a separate piece of paper have him write down the same number. He will then sign his name next to the number." (The signature sheet)

If necessary, you will sign an affidavit that the number on the statement represents a real person known to you. Let him know that if Wilbert is arrested and there is a trial, he may have to testify anyway." I called Loren. I told him everything the sheriff had said. I asked him if he would do it. He said he would like to talk to his friends first.

I suggested that we all meet together. That way I could tell everyone what the sheriff had said. I also told him to tell his friends that I would do nothing without their knowledge or consent.

A few days later he called. His friends had agreed to meet with me. He wondered if tonight would be okay.

I said it would. At about 8:00 p.m., five young people, all about Loren's age, appeared at the door. Most of them I had never seen before. Some were clearly nervous.

I thanked them for coming and told them to relax. They were not required to do anything. Also, I would not do anything without their prior approval. I then related what the sheriff had offered. I told them that there was a possibility that if it went to trial, they would be required to testify. I also told them that as difficult as it may be, it was important that they do the right thing. I then left them alone to make their decision. About an hour later Loren came out. He said they had decided.

When I came back and sat down another young person (Bret) took over. He was obviously their leader. "We will do it," he said. That night five boys gave their statements. Some were long, some short; some were detailed, some less so. Some wrote of their involvement with Wilbert, some not. All indicated that Wilbert was a sexual predator.

I thanked the boys and told them how proud I was of them. On a separate sheet of paper, I had written the numbers 1 through 5 in a column. I asked them to sign their names next to the numbers. The number next to their signature was to be written on their statement. They all did as requested.

The next morning the sheriff picked up the statements. He did not take the signature sheet. Nor did he ask me for an affidavit. That evening the sheriff called. They had arrested Wilbert.

"You ought to see what we got," he said.

"What?" I asked.

Wilbert had kept a diary of all his "clients" as he called them, and all their "activities." He had Polaroid pictures. He had also hidden a tape recorder in his bedroom.

"I'm calling to tell you that the names of some of your kids may be in the diary. Do you want to tell me who they are, now that I have their names anyway?"

"No," I answered, "But who do you think they are?"

He gave me a number of names. In the background I could hear him turn pages that I took to be the diary. Some of the boys' names were in the diary. Others were not. Two names shocked me. I knew them. The names did not belong to any of the boys. They were Jeffrey and Tanya Hickens.

"Sheriff," I said, "I will ask the boys if they will talk to you. By the way, when did the Hickens see Wilbert?"

He gave me a date. "That may not be the only time," he said, "I haven't seen everything."

I was curious, "What did they do?"

He laughed, "I can't give you the details, pastor, but suffice it to say that they did a good job of satisfying each other. Let's just call it a "three-ring circus." He laughed again.

I called Loren. I told him what the sheriff had told me. I asked him if he or any of the friends would agree to talk to the sheriff, given that some of their names were in the diary anyway. He asked me whose names were in the diary. I told him I wasn't sure, which was technically true. I didn't know if the sheriff had given me all the names. Furthermore, he hadn't seen everything yet. Loren said he would get back to me. He later called. Neither he nor any of his friends wanted to do anything more.

The Hickens had been coming to our church. They had asked to see me and when I met with them, they talked about how impressed they were with our church. They were considering joining. Before I left he asked that we pray together, which was unusual.

I checked my appointment book. I had seen them a week after their "three-ring circus."

At first I was angry. "Just another hypocrite," I thought. But wait, we had met after they had seen Wilbert. Perhaps it wasn't as satisfying as the sheriff had said. Maybe they did want to change. I would give them the benefit of any doubt. After all Christ did not come to save those who were already righteous.

Wilbert was out on bail. Time passed and I heard nothing. In the meantime there had been an election. A different sheriff and District Attorney had been elected. I called the new sheriff. He said he didn't know what

I was talking about. I then called the District Attorney but he refused to talk to me. Duke (the bar tender) later told me that the case against Wilbert had been dropped. Apparently no one was prepared to testify. I was angry and discouraged, but it did not matter. By that time, I had pretty much decided to leave the ministry.

CHAPTER 6
WHY I LEFT THE MINISTRY

Being a pastor means caring for the needs of the congregation, visiting, evangelizing, teaching, preaching, preparing two sermons a week and attending meetings. The full-time obligation to my family remained.

For reasons that will eventually become clear, I soon began to question some of the doctrines of our denomination. While preparing sermons or teaching catechism, I often bumped into these doctrines. Initially I attempted to put these questions out of my mind, but they persisted. In the short term doubts or questions can be ignored, but until dealt with, they continue to fester. It was important that I know. I was a preacher. In my heart there was a rule (like a second golden rule): "When you ask someone to accept what you say, you must know that what you say is true."

Over time I came to believe that there were some doctrines that I could *not* agree with. As such could I even remain a pastor of that church? So I decided to deal with it. I began to keep notes on those doctrines I found most troubling.

There are three "Doctrinal Standards" which were adopted by our denomination. These "Standards" are interpretations of Scripture that our denomination had accepted as correct. As such, they are binding on all office bearers including pastors. These "Doctrinal Standards" are:

1. The Confession of Faith (1561),

2. The Heidelberg Catechism (1563),

3. The Canons of Dort (1618-19).

I had no issues with the Heidelberg Catechism, which I believe is a reasonably accurate summary of the Gospel. My only issues were with the Confession of Faith and especially the Canons of Dort. I will summarize some of the doctrines contained in these "Standards." To the extent possible, I will use the actual words. Some of the words are archaic, and some of the sentences can be long and convoluted. I have simplified where possible, but please bear with me. You may be surprised by what they say. It marked the beginning of the end of my ministry.

When I was ordained into the ministry, I was required to sign a Form of Subscription. The form provides that those who sign it *"declare by this our subscription that we heartily believe and are persuaded that all the articles and points of doctrine contained in the Confession..., together with the explanation of some points of the aforesaid doctrine made by the National Synod of Dordrecht, 1618-19, do fully agree with the Word of God."*

"We promise therefore diligently to teach and faithfully to defend the aforesaid doctrine, without either directly or indirectly contradicting the same by our public preaching or writing."

The Confession of Faith – The Belgic Confession

The "Confession" referred to above is the "Confession of Faith," the oldest Doctrinal Standard of the Christian Reformed Church. It was written by Guido de Bres in 1561. He was a pastor of a Reformed church in the Netherlands. It is often referred to as the Belgic

Confession because it was written in a region now known as Belgium.

What does the Confession teach?

"We believe that through the disobedience of Adam, original sin is extended to all mankind; which is a corruption of the whole nature and a hereditary disease, wherewith even infants in their mother's womb are infected, and which produces in man all sorts of sin, being in him as a root thereof, and therefore is so vile and abominable in the sight of God that it is sufficient to condemn all mankind" (Article XV).

In fact, people are so dead in sin that even wanting good is impossible (Article XIV).

Because we are so "vile and abominable" salvation is necessary (Article XVII).

But salvation is limited only to those whom God from the beginning elected (Article XVI).

So who are the elect? Only those in whom "the Holy Spirit kindles...an upright faith" (Article XXII).

And in whom are we to have this "upright faith?" In Jesus Christ "being conceived in the womb of the blessed virgin Mary by the power of the Holy Spirit, without the means of man;" and who did..."assume human nature...

so as to save both body and soul" (Article XVIII).

And what will happen to those whose hearts the Holy Spirit chose not to kindle? First their souls will be "joined and united with their proper bodies in which they formerly lived." Then they will "be tormented in the eternal fire" (Article XXXVII).

And how do we know all this to be true? "Because the Holy Spirit witnesses in our hearts that they are from God, and also because they carry the evidence thereof in themselves" (Article V).

The Canons of Dort

The doctrines adopted by the National Reformed Synod of Dordrecht in 1618-19, referred to in the Form of Subscription are called the "Canons of Dort." Many theologians have summarized the Canons under various doctrinal heads using the familiar acronym "TULIP:" Total depravity, Unconditional election, Limited atonement, Irresistible grace and Perseverance of the saints. All of the doctrines represented by the acronym TULIP, when taken together, form the constituent parts of the doctrine of election. However, as with the previous Confession of Faith, I prefer to summarize the Canons using the actual words to the extent possible.

What do the Canons teach?
The "First Head of Doctrine" teaches:

"All men have sinned in Adam...and are deserving of eternal death" (Article 1; total depravity).

"The wrath of God abides upon those who believe not this gospel" (Article 4).

"Faith in Jesus Christ and salvation through Him is the free gift of God" (Article 5).

In fact, some may not even want this gift but "He graciously softens the hearts of the elect, however obstinate, and inclines them to believe" (Article 6; irresistible grace).

"Election is the unchangeable purpose of God, whereby, before the foundation of the world He has...chosen from the whole human race...a certain number of persons to redemption in Christ." Those who are elected are "by nature neither better nor more deserving than others" (Article 7; unconditional election).

"This election was not founded upon foreseen faith...or any other good quality or disposition in man" (Article 9; unconditional election).

Rather, "The good pleasure of God is the sole cause of this gracious election" (Article 10; unconditional election).

"Nothing can change the good pleasure of God" (Article

11; unconditional election).

In fact, some may not even know that they were elected. "The elect in due time, though in various degrees and in different measures, attain the assurance of their eternal and unchangeable election" (Article 12: unconditional election).

"Election is the express testimony of sacred scripture that not all, but some only, are elected, while others are passed by in the eternal decree." As for those not elected, God will "condemn and punish them forever" (Article 15; unconditional election).

"The children of believers are holy, not by nature, but in virtue of the covenant of grace (and) godly parents ought not to doubt the election and salvation of their children" (Article 17; unconditional election).

When taken together the necessary implications of the foregoing articles are:

1. Of those people whom God himself created; some are chosen (the elect), and some are not (the reprobates).

2. Those who are chosen will experience eternal bliss (heaven). Those who are not chosen will experience eternal torment (hell).

3. The criterion for selection is *solely* the good pleasure of God. It has nothing to do with

those selected or rejected. Those rejected were no more worthy of hell than were the selected. The reprobates are discarded not because they rejected the offer of salvation. No offer was ever made. They were discarded simply because they were not selected.

4. In other words, through no fault of their own, there will be some (whom God himself created), who will suffer eternal damnation. There will be others (although no more worthy) who will have their names picked. They are the winners in the cosmic lottery. And the prize is fantastic. It is eternal life. Further, Article 11 states that the lottery has already been held; the names have been drawn; and the prizes awarded. Nothing can be changed.

The "Second Head of Doctrine" teaches:

"Sin committed...should be punished, not only with temporal but with eternal punishments, both in body and soul" (Article 1).

Christ was sent as an atonement for sin. Although His atonement was sufficient for all, it was limited to "those only who were from eternity chosen" (Article 8; limited atonement).

The "Third and Fourth Heads of Doctrine" teach:

As a result of Adam's sin people "became wicked, rebellious, and obdurate" (Article 1; total depravity).

"Man after the fall begat children in his own likeness. A corrupt stock produced a corrupt offspring" (Article 2; total depravity).

"Therefore all men are conceived in sin, and are by nature children of wrath, incapable of saving good, prone to evil, dead in sin, and in bondage thereto" (Article 3; total depravity).

Given that people are completely dead in sin there cannot be a "proper exercise of free will" (Article 10; total depravity).

Consequently, it is the Holy Spirit who "opens the closed and softens the hardened heart and...infuses new qualities into the will" (Article 11; irresistible grace).

This quickening enables one to believe (Article 13;

irresistible grace).

"Faith is therefore to be considered as a gift of God....
Because it is in reality conferred upon him, breathed and
infused into him." In fact, God "produces both the will to
believe and the act of believing" (Article 14; irresistible
grace).

And so that there be no confusion "man can have no
hope of being able to rise from his fall by his own free
will" (Article 16; total depravity).

The foregoing articles provide that people are so
vile that they cannot even will to change. Only God provides that will. Once the will to change has been infused,
then the means to change (namely, faith) is also provided
by God. The elect are not selected because they of their
own free will accepted the offer of salvation. No offer
was ever made because people in their natural state have
no capacity to accept it. The elect were simply given the
gift of salvation. Those who won the greatest lottery
ever, i.e., salvation, were not even capable of wanting to
win it.

The "Fifth Head of Doctrine" teaches:

Once a Christian, always a Christian. "God is faithful,

who, having conferred grace, mercifully confirms and powerfully preserves them therein, even to the end" (Article 3; perseverance of the saints).

God "confirms and preserves true believers in a state of grace," even though people are drawn "into great and heinous sins...sometimes by the righteous permission of God" (Article 4; perseverance of the saints).

"The carnal mind is unable to comprehend this doctrine of the perseverance of the saints and the certainty thereof" (Article 15).

Consider the implications of this last head of doctrine, which deals with the perseverance of the saints. Article 17 of the first head of doctrine asserts that the children of the elect are also elect. Given that they are preserved as such through an infusion of faith, they can never be anything but Christian. All of their children will then also be preserved as Christians, as will their children, ad infinitum. In other words, none of the children, or grandchildren, or great-grandchildren etc., can ever lose their faith. Why would parents pray for their children's spiritual wellbeing, when their ultimate wellbeing is already assured?

The Standards

When I look back, I wonder how I was able to serve the church as long as I did (1970-73). Even then I thought the church should take another look at these standards. Now I am even more convinced.

The Standards were all written between 1561 and 1619. Sinful people wrote them all; the Holy Spirit inspired none. None were infallible, and neither did they claim to be. Most were written to refute a group or heresy at that time. For example, in respect to the Trinity, the Confession of Faith states: "This doctrine of the Holy Trinity has always been affirmed...against...heretics, as Marcion, Manes, Praxeas, Sabellius, Samosutenus, Arius, and such like, who have been justly condemned" (Article IX).

In other articles the Confession condemns "the Sadducees, the Manichees, the damnable error of the Epicureans, the Pelagians...and we detest the Anabaptists and other seditious people."

Whenever a doctrine seeks to refute another doctrine (the alleged heresy), then the emphasis is always on that which differentiates the doctrine from the so-called heresy. Those beliefs that are common to both are never highlighted, even though the common beliefs may form the bulk of what both parties believe. It is like two political parties. In an effort to acquire votes, that which distinquishes them is always emphasized, but that which is shared is suppressed. Issues are selected and facts are spun to support a position already taken. Context is ignored and perspective is lost. Positions harden and words often become intemperate as was the case with the Confession. This leads to polarization and extremism on both sides. Over the years I have learned that the whole truth is seldom found in the extremes.

The History of the Canons of Dort

Some history may be helpful. Jacob Arminius (1560-1609) was a professor of theology at the University of Leyden in the Netherlands. He did not accept the doctrine of election as provided for in the Confession of Faith written by Pastor Guido de Bres. One year after the death of Arminius in 1609, his followers (called the Remonstrants) circulated a position paper articulating their differences with the Confession. The Calvinists sided with Pastor de Bres and almost all the other denominational groups, including the Lutherans, sided with the Remonstrants.

What further complicated matters was that during this time the Dutch were in the middle of an eighty year war for independence from Spain (1568 --1649). In 1609 a truce was called which lasted until 1621, after which war resumed. Many of the Dutch military and political leaders were Calvinists.

In his writings Calvin had departed from the orthodox position that the powers that be are ordained by God. He defended the right of people to fight against oppressive governments, that the Dutch perceived Spain to be. Encouraged by Calvin's writings the Calvinists were fiercely patriotic. Inevitably, patriotism and theology began to mix.

The Remonstrants also opposed the Spanish occupation, but they were less vociferous. As a result they were perceived to be sympathetic to Spain. In fact, during this time some remonstrant leaders were arrested for treason. The conflict between the two groups became so hateful and divisive that it almost led to civil war.

Consequently, at the urging of the Dutch government, the Reformed Churches of the Netherlands held a Synod in the Dutch Reformed Church in the city of Dordrecht in 1618-1619. There were 99 voting delegates — all men. The Synod held 154 sessions over a period of seven months. Initially thirteen Remonstrants were seated. Under the leadership of the moderator, Johannes Bogerman, the thirteen Remonstrants were dismissed. Some delegates were upset by Bogermans's conduct, but no steps were taken to rectify the wrong. All the remaining delegates were from the Calvinist side, and hence were predisposed in favor of the Confession. (So much for due process.)

Ostensibly, the question to be considered was whether the Doctrines of Arminius could be reconciled with the Confession. It is clear, however, that the question was only a pretence to fairness. Everyone knew there could be no reconciliation. In fact, the absence of reconciliation was the reason the Synod was called in the first place. The real purpose was to refute the Remonstrants.

Once the thirteen Remonstrants were dismissed and there being no one left to speak for them, matters moved quickly. Not surprising, the remaining 86 delegates all voted against the Remonstrants. They had accomplished their purpose.

The Canons were born out of a bitter conflict. Due process was obviously not followed. The results were determined by partisan politics and yet they are binding on our church. All office bearers are required to sign allegiance.

When I first read the Canons I was dismayed. It is true that I was aware in a general sense what these doctrinal Standards were. But I had no idea that I would be required to sign a form promising "diligently to teach and faithfully defend" these doctrines.

As I attempted to work my way through the Canons,

Winson Elgersma

my doubts as to their truth began to grow. Increasingly, I came to believe that most of the doctrines are to some extent false. I wondered how I could remain a minister in the Christian Reformed Church.

Form of Subscription

I believe that the seminary failed in their duty to their students. On the very first day of class the students should have been told that, if they wished to become pastors, they would be required to sign the "Form of Subscription." The form provides that "we heartily believe" in the Standards. We should then have been told what the various Standards purport. I believe that if that had been done, some of the students may have left while they still could.

But that was not done; instead, there was incremental creep. There were language classes and history classes. There were classes in which scriptural interpretation and doctrine were taught, discussed and occasionally debated. But there was not one class on the Standards themselves. Neither were we told that we would be required to sign a Form of Subscription by which we agreed to be bound by the doctrines contained in the Standards.

It was not until we moved to Iowa that I even knew a form existed which I would be required to sign. I had thought that my training at Calvin Seminary had qualified me to interpret Scripture. I had assumed that the Seminary's recommendation to the Synod, and the Synod's recommendation to the churches, had affirmed my qualifications to interpret Scripture. If not, then why were these recommendations made? Conversely, if the recommendations did affirm my qualifications to interpret Scripture, then why would an additional form be necessary?

Instead, I found that I was bound by various interpretations of Scripture written by people in 1561 and 1618. Furthermore, these people were no more qualified to interpret Scripture than was I. The author of the Confession was a pastor in a church, just as I was.

I was surprised that I was required through the form to state: "We heartily believe and are persuaded that all the articles and points of doctrine...do fully agree with the Word of God," and "We promise therefore diligently to teach and faithfully defend the aforesaid doctrine."

By the time I was fully aware of the implications of the form, it was too late. Signing under "protest" was not an option. Three or four years were already invested. Money had to be made and children had to be fed.

Perhaps I was the only one who did not know that

I would be required to sign the form. I do not know. But I do know this – I was not the only one to disagree with the Doctrinal Standards. I know there are certainly some (perhaps many) ministers serving the church who do *not* believe in the doctrinal interpretations provided in the Standards. I have spoken with some.

As such, they are required to spin, modify or curtail their message for fear of contradiction with the Standards. The message then becomes weak and without substance. Preaching with conviction is lost. But it is not just the message that suffers. So do the messengers. To a certain extent they become hypocrites. They pretend to uphold a doctrine, which in their heart they cannot support. They live in a perpetual state of deceit. Truth, honesty, certainty and candor become casualties. Deceit is like a disease. It compromises the person. The answers to certain questions must now be massaged, resulting in half-truths or worse. Enthusiasm is lost.

The merits of the Canons of Dort

Essentially the Canons of Dort are a treatise on the doctrine of election. I disagreed then, and I disagree now, with; (1) the doctrine of election, and (2) the correlate doctrine that we have no free will. Both of these doctrines were, on their own, sufficient cause for me to leave the ministry.

In summary, the doctrine of election teaches that all people on the face of the earth (whom God Himself created) are thoroughly and equally wicked. As a result all are in need of salvation, even though none want it. Despite the people's desire to the contrary, God decides to save a few (the elect), but not others (the reprobates). It isn't as if God offered salvation to all and the elect accepted, while the reprobates rejected it. No offers were made. God simply chose some and not others. No criteria were used as the basis for selection. Those whom God chose not to save He further condemns in the final judgment and punishes them with "eternal fire," even though they were no more deserving of punishment than those whom He chose to save.

If the doctrine of election were true, would not the final judgment be a sham? Would not God be punishing people for His choices, rather than for theirs?

An analogy may be helpful. Assume that we all have many children. We have taken them on a cruise, but the cruise ship sinks. We have found a lifeboat that is large enough to accommodate all our children including the babies. All are in equal need of rescue. We have the time and the capacity to save them all, but we choose to save only a few. The few we save are no more worthy of rescue than those we choose not to save. Those whom

147

we choose not to save, including babies, we further punish with "eternal torment."

If parents did as described above, we would all be horrified at such an injustice. We would consider such behavior revolting, repulsive and reprehensible. We would call for retribution. Is it more acceptable if we attribute such behavior to our Heavenly Father? Ought we not to be ashamed of ourselves even to think it, let alone teach it?

Surely, the offer of rescue (salvation) is made to all the drowning children. For whatever reason, there may be those who choose not to be rescued, but at least they had the choice. When they drown it will not be because the father (God) failed to throw the rescue rope to them, but rather because the children chose not to seize it.

Someone once said that John 3:16 is the gospel in a capsule. "For God so loved the world, that He gave His only begotten Son, that whosoever believes in Him should not perish, but have eternal life." I know that there are some ministers who have tried to pound the round peg of "John 3:16" into the square hole of "election." But I believe, that without a magician's contortion the two cannot be honestly reconciled.

Most Christian churches do not, and would not, accept the foregoing doctrines. Of all of the Christians in the world, those who hold the doctrine of election to be true are a small minority. Furthermore, if we were to canvass the members of the Christian Reformed Church, that small minority would be smaller still. I know that truth is not measured by numbers, but is it not a factor that ought to be considered? Do we (the few) have the truth that has eluded the many?

As I was struggling to find a solution, I spoke to two neighboring pastors.

One pastor could not remember reading either the Confession or the Canons. He was however, familiar with the doctrines contained in the Canons, and particularly with the doctrine of election. I asked him if he accepted the doctrine of election as true?

"Are you kidding?" he answered.

I asked him how he could sign the Form of Subscription, given that he did not accept "election" as true.

His response was interesting. He said that he grew up in the Christian Reformed Church. When he came to realize that he wanted to be a pastor, it did not occur to him to do ministry anywhere else. He took the position that signing the form was a meaningless formality.

It was also his opinion that the doctrine of election was only one of many doctrines. These other doctrines included baptism, the virgin birth, and the ascension of Christ among others. He believed that I was attributing a greater value to the doctrine of election than it deserved.

The other pastor had read the Standards. He was

clearly ambivalent about the doctrine of election. He felt that there was much to be said on both sides. He was also of the opinion that the doctrine of election was only a small part of what the church stood for. I asked him why he would want to be a pastor, if the doctrine of election were true. After all, God had already decided which of his children he would save.

He said that although God knew whom he would save, we do not know. It is the pastor's duty to let people know that they may be saved, and to accept the means by which they could claim the gift of salvation, namely through the death and resurrection of Christ.

I told him that the doctrine of election made it clear that no one has the capacity to claim the gift of salvation. God must first infuse that capacity. He acknowledged that was a problem for him. He said that it had bothered him when he signed the form, but because he wasn't sure, he signed it anyway.

Several years after I left the ministry, he also left. I do not know whether his half-hearted endorsement of the Standards had become a half-hearted rejection, or whether that had anything to do with his departure. I do know that it troubled him that he could not give his whole-hearted support, especially since he had promised to diligently teach the very doctrines he now questioned.

I was more in line with the first pastor, in that I had come to the conclusion that "election" was false. As such,

I was left with a very personal decision: could I continue in the ministry, despite my firm conviction that some of the doctrines I had promised to teach were in fact false? I mean no disrespect to the pastors who decided that they could continue. I know how difficult the decision is, but I decided that I could not.

I do not believe it necessary to say anything more about the merits (or the lack thereof) of the doctrine of election. The Standards speak for themselves.

In particular I have no desire to marshal Scripture verses and fire them at those who accept the doctrine of election. I find such religious battles to be unhelpful.

In fact, such religious battles have already been fought, and in my view they accomplished nothing. Pastor Guido de Bres selected his Biblical verses and the Remonstrants responded with theirs. The Synod of Dordrecht then selected even more verses in support of Guido de Bres.

The religious wars only succeeded in raising the level of hatred and hostility and many people died. In fact, four days after the Synod concluded their deliberations with prayer, one remonstrant was beheaded. I believe the problem was that all parties selected verses that supported a position already taken. In those circumstances the Bible can be made to say anything.

The better approach is to assess whether a particular doctrine fits within the whole of the Gospel message.

In this case does the doctrine of election make sense in the context of the entire Gospel story including for example the ten commandments, the great commission and the final judgment? What is the sense in saying "you shall not murder, commit adultery, steal or lie," when on our own we have no capacity to do anything different? And what is the point of the great commission "go and make disciples of all nations..." when such disciples were already chosen from eternity past, and the making of these disciples is solely and entirely in the hands of God? And where is the justice in the final judgment when some are sentenced to "be tormented in the eternal fire," for choices not of their own making?

I leave it to you the reader to decide on the merits. Do you believe that you have no free will? Do you believe that God welcomes some of his children but discards others based on nothing other than His so-called "good pleasure?" If you do, then why is there a judgment? In fact, why is preaching, teaching or missions even necessary?

A New Form of Subscription

Then in 2005 there was hope. A church in Surrey, B.C., asked the Synod of the Christian Reformed Church to consider changing the Form of Subscription because many individuals would no longer sign it. The Synod agreed and recommended that the form be revised. The grounds for the recommendation were:

A. The survey conducted among the churches indicates that a substantial number of the churches believe that an update is desirable.

B. The present Form of Subscription contains statements that are subject to misinterpretation.

C. A more contemporary expression of agreement will make the requirement more meaningful.

A study committee was appointed to implement the recommendation (Acts of Synod 2005, p. 735). In 2008 the study committee reported back to Synod. In their report they concluded that a new form would require more than a rewrite. Rather it would require a study of the role of our "Confessions" in our Church. Their report was received, but not adopted. A new committee was formed.

In 2012 the new committee reported back to Synod, with a new Form of Subscription. The new form was titled "Covenant for Office Bearers in the Christian

Reformed Church." In part, the new form states:

> *"We also affirm three confessions – the Belgic Confession, the Heidelberg Catechism, and the Canons of Dort – as historic Reformed expressions of the Christian faith whose doctrines fully agree with the Word of God. These confessions continue to define the way we understand Scripture, direct the way we live in response to the gospel, and locate us within the larger body of Christ.*

> *Grateful for these expressions of faith, we promise to be formed and governed by them. We heartily believe and will promote and defend their doctrines faithfully, conforming our preaching, teaching, writing, serving, and living to them." [Italics added]*

In their report the committee acknowledged that they "attempted to write a Form of Subscription even for those who do not think we should have such a document, because several of the responses raised points in that direction" (p. 4). There was virtually no discussion "about the role of the Confessions in our denomination," as recommended be the previous committee.

Nonetheless, the new form was adopted by Synod. Furthermore, as with the previous form, it is "to be signed by professors, ministers, commissioned pastors, elders, and deacons when ordained and/or installed in office."

It is clear from even a casual reading that the new form isn't new at all. It is simply a rewrite of the old form. Anyone who was unable to sign the old form will also find the new form to be unacceptable.

It is important to note that neither the old nor the new form permits cherry picking. In other words a pastor is not free to heartily believe and promote those doctrines contained in the Standards that he or she believes conform to Scripture. It is all or nothing. Specifically, anyone signing the new form asserts that all of the doctrines contained in the Confession and Cannons "fully agree with the Word of God" and therefore we promise to conform our preaching, teaching and writing to these doctrines.

Neither pastor whom I had consulted fully endorsed the doctrine of election. Nonetheless, both signed the form because they believed that the doctrine was only a "small part" of what the church stands for.

Clearly this opinion was not shared by the authors of the new form. They obviously felt that the doctrine of election was such an important "expression of faith" that it should exclude from service those who do not agree with it.

So what is it: a small part of what the church stands for, or an important expression of faith sufficient to exclude office bearers from service?

If the doctrine of election is as important as the new form makes it out to be, then the Seminary failed in their duty (not only to their students as previously indicated) but also to the church at large, by not providing a course dedicated exclusively to the Standards. Such a course would enable their graduates (when preaching) to properly formulate the "expression of faith" in conformity to the Standards as required by the form. Such a course would be especially important given that their graduates are required to promise; "We heartily believe and will promote and defend" all the doctrines contained in the Standards because they all "fully agree with the Word of God."

And what is the church to do with those pastors already ordained who do not "fully" or "heartily agree" with the doctrine of election? Obviously they cannot fulfill their obligation arising out of the form, that is to "promote and defend" a doctrine that they do not accept.

And what about the other office bearers -- the elders and deacons? The form requires that they make the same promises and therefore incur the same obligations. Given that one obligation is to "promote and defend" the doctrine of election as described in the Canons, then shouldn't the form also provide that all potential office bearers NOT sign the form unless they have actually read the Canons?

On the other hand, if the doctrine of election is only a small part of what the church stands for (which I think most people believe) then why should that small part exclude those office bearers who would otherwise happily serve the church? If it is only a small part then by definition there must be a larger part. And doesn't this larger part represent what most of us believe? Is not this "small part" akin to the issue raised by the man in Pella when he asked about "women in office?" The issue was a small part, but through it the speaker intended to separate me from him. Yet when confronted by the greater part (the Apostles Creed) he acknowledged our togetherness. When measured by the impact on the daily lives of church members, the issue of women in office is probably more important than the doctrine of election. So why not drop the Form of Subscription, the effect of which is to separate us based on a "small part", and fashion a new more inclusive form? Why not accept office bearers who share with us the much greater part? Undoubtedly the church will benefit by their participation.

The status of the Belgic Confession and the Canons of Dort

At this point I wish to deal with the status accorded to the Belgic Confession and the Canons of Dort as compared to the Scripture. In respect to the Scripture the form provides that "we submit to it in all matters of life and faith." But in respect to the Confession and the Canons the form provides that these "doctrines fully agree with the Word of God" and further that "we heartily believe and will promote and defend their doctrines faithfully, conforming our preaching, teaching, writing, serving and living to them."

Without doubt, the form has elevated an interpretation of Scripture (the Confession and the Canons and hence the doctrine of election) to the same level as Scripture and perhaps even higher when assessed by what is required from us. Attributing such an elevated status to the Confession and the Canons is entirely inappropriate. Would it not have been better if the only requirement for office bearers was that they submit to the Scriptures in all matters of life and faith and that they conform their preaching, teaching, writing, serving and living to it?

Another analogy may be helpful. Scripture is to the church what the American Constitution is to the United

States. Every member of Congress (an office bearer) must swear or affirm that "I will support and defend the Constitution... and that I will bear true faith and allegiance to the same...." Every President (an office bearer) must swear or affirm that I "will to the best of my ability, preserve, protect and defend the Constitution...." None of the oaths provide that in addition to defending the constitution the office bearer must also agree with and defend the various interpretations provided by the Supreme Court and rightly so. That way even those who disagree with the Court's decisions can still be office bearers and serve their country in that capacity. If the oaths for political office were as the Form of Subscription now is, then all political office bearers would be required to agree with Roe vs. Wade as a prerequisite to service. (Roe vs. Wade was the Supreme Court case that permitted unrestricted abortions in the first three months.) Whether you agree or disagree with the interpretations, it is inappropriate to raise the interpretation of a document to the same level as the document itself and in so doing exclude those who wish to serve.

Yet that is exactly what our church has done. We compel our office bearers to defend not only Scripture, but also an interpretation of Scripture written about 450 years ago by sinful men in questionable circumstances. Those who do not accept the interpretation, but who do accept Scripture cannot serve the church as an office bearer. Even those who agree with the doctrine of election should object.

Furthermore, does not the new form contradict the very Confessional Standards that it purports to support? Article VII of the Belgic Confession states: "Neither may we consider any writing of men, however holy these men may have been, of equal value with those divine Scriptures."

To raise the interpretation of Scripture to the same level as Scripture is in my view, the Old Testament equivalent of a "graven image." The new form requires all office bearers "to promote and defend" the Belgic Confession and the Canons of Dort, "conforming our preaching, teaching, writing, serving and living to them." Is this not a commitment that ought to be made exclusively to Scripture?

Conclusion

I know that there are many articles and books that spin the Belgic Confession and the Canons of Dort in such a way as to make them more acceptable, but please read them for yourself. It wasn't until I read them that I realized what a mistake I had made when I signed the Form of Subscription which compelled me to defend them.

If you agree that office bearers should not be compelled to conform their "preaching, teaching, writing, serving and living" to the Belgic Confession and the Canons of Dort, rather than to the Scripture, please let your local church know. Insist that every office bearer read these documents. I know from experience that falsehood flourishes in the darkness of an uninformed mind. Perhaps even study groups on the Confession and the Canons would be helpful.

In writing this chapter, there are two results I am hopeful for. I am hopeful that the Christian Reformed Church will reconsider "the role of our Confessions in our Church" which the 2008 synodical committee wisely suggested. At the very least I hope that the Church will drop the Form of Subscription as it now is, and in so doing allow space for those many Christian office bearers who love the Church, but do not wish to pledge allegiance to the so-called Confessional Standards.

CHAPTER 7
REAL ESTATE

When I notified my parents of my decision to leave the ministry I knew that they would be disappointed but I did not realize the depth of their disappointment until they called. They implored me to reconsider. I said my mind was made up. We then received a letter. They made it clear that they had expected better.

We had virtually no savings. We lived rent free in the parsonage, but our annual salary was only $6,000. If no ministry, what then? We had three children. How could I support them?

We had initially intended to go to Edmonton. However, given my parents' letter, we decided to check out Toronto. Neither of us had been there before. I would go in advance, to explore both the rental and job market. I had arranged to see some friends to discuss the job market. The next day would be spent with a real estate agent. The job market was promising. The rental market was a different story.

The real estate agent had pre-scheduled some lower-priced homes and apartments near downtown. They were far too expensive. Throughout the day we proceeded further from downtown. Because I get motion sickness when riding in the passenger seat, we took my car. Most of the time I had no idea where we were.

By late afternoon we had not yet found anything. What was affordable was either too small or too filthy. We were both discouraged. He went back to his office but I do not remember how. I know that I did not drive him back. I was left to find a place to eat and an affordable motel. I wanted to spend as little as possible, given how little we had.

I checked a few motels, but they were too expensive. I then saw a small sign. I believe all it said was "beds." It was in the window of what looked like an older home. Good, I thought. It looks cheap. I parked in front of the house and walked in. The interior was in better condition than the exterior. There were no signs that indicated a reception desk. There were only some closets along one side and some pictures on the other. On the far side was a counter. In front of the counter were two or three chairs around a coffee table. Standing beside the counter was a well-dressed older lady. Behind her was a sign: "Park behind the building."

"I need a room," I said. "How much?"

She looked at me. She then walked to the window and looked at my car. "You from Iowa?" she asked, although it was more of a statement than a question.

"Yes," I answered. I told her that we were thinking about moving to Toronto, and that I had been looking for an apartment. "I need a room," I said again.

"For how long?" she responded.

"For the night."

"Are you alone?"

"Yes."

"With or without?" she asked.

I had no idea what she was talking about. I thought it might be a private bathroom.

"With," I said.

She rang a little press bell. "Louise here will help you," she said, pointing to a lady coming from an adjoining room.

"Hi sweetie," Louise said, taking me by the arm. "I'll show you what's available." We went into the room that she had come from. There were three ladies, all about my age, in various stages of undress.

I then realized what the "with" was. I had walked into a brothel. I didn't even know they existed in Canada.

I had to get out. I told her that my car was parked out front. I wanted to move it to the back before it was ticketed.

"That's fine, sweetie," she said, "we will be here."

I drove all night. During the night I decided to have a little talk with myself. There were several other times that my bravado had gotten me in trouble. One was the incident in Tulsa.

Another was when we were still in seminary. We had cared for the Slater children to enable the parents to enjoy a weekend together. They paid us back by taking our children. Joyce and I decided to begin the weekend by going for dinner at an upscale restaurant. When we sat down the waiter asked if we would like a drink.

"Yes," I said, "I'll have a scotch." I had never ordered a drink in a restaurant before, but I had seen a movie once where the man had ordered a scotch. I wanted Joyce to think that I knew something about the ways of the world; that I was sophisticated.

"How would you like it?" he asked. I sat in stunned silence. I didn't know that there were different ways to like it. Furthermore, he wasn't providing any options. On my own, I could come up with nothing. I could feel the façade of sophistication being stripped away. It was painful. I said nothing. "How would you like it?" the waiter repeated.

I was beginning to panic. Then I remembered the

man in the movie. He had ordered scotch on the rocks. "On the rocks," I said quickly. He brought the drink. It was less than I expected. I gulped it down in one swallow. The pain had now become physical. Not only did I not know how to order a scotch, I also didn't know how to drink it. I began to cough. I couldn't stop. My throat was burning and my eyes were tearing. The waiter asked if I was all right.

"Yes," I managed to say, but I wasn't. I went to the bathroom. I continued to cough. I drank some cold water, which helped. When I came back my voice was hoarse. The waiter couldn't understand me when I gave him my food order. He had to ask three times. I had wanted to be urbane, but ended up looking and sounding like a bumpkin.

I tried to identify the insecurities that motivated my behavior. Perhaps it was the fear of ridicule, or conversely the need for approval. I wasn't sure. But one thing I knew: whatever the reason I had to stop pretending that I knew something when I didn't. I resolved to simply acknowledge my ignorance and limitations. I had always been a bit of a "show-off." That would have to change. I had to accept who I was, including my warts. Years earlier I was humiliated when I tried to change my laugh. I thought I had learned but apparently not. It occurred to me that we may be the only creatures on earth who refuse to be who we are.

Unfortunately, my insecurities were not just causing problems, but they were also depriving me of opportunities. When I was in high school, I was a fairly good basketball player, at least by local standards. But when I went to college I didn't even try-out for the team. I had heard that basketball was big in Iowa. I didn't want to try and then face the disgrace of failure. It wasn't until I watched the team play that I realized I had missed an opportunity.

While we were still in the ministry, Joyce and I had gone on a camping trip with some friends (Dan and Donna) to a lake in Minnesota. During that trip Dan had talked about how much he loved hunting. He said that he would go into the bush and build a blind in some tree. He would stock it with some food and then for about a week he would live in it, by himself. He said that he spent the week reviewing the past year of his life, and he thought about how he could be a better person in the future. He referred to that experience as his birthday. It was the one time each year that he took inventory of himself.

When I look back now, I realize that the trip home from Toronto was my birthday. By the time I reached home I was a year older.

* * * * *

Edmonton would be more affordable but moving is

difficult when money is an issue. We explored all options. Crossing the border with a rental truck was very expensive. The reason was that a truck rented in the United States could not be left in Canada. In the end, we concluded that the least expensive option was to move our possessions by truck to Kenora, Ontario; then from Kenora to Edmonton by rail. The truck could then be returned to Minneapolis.

We made arrangements with the Canadian National Railway to purchase a one-way ticket to Edmonton, for one half of a rail car. However, when I arrived in Kenora, they refused to accept my motorcycle. Eventually they agreed providing that I could empty the gas tank. From our belongings, I was able to find a hose and a pail. Then in the presence of a railway inspector, I siphoned the gas into the pail and poured it into the truck. Once all the belongings were in, they sealed the door and gave me a key.

Joyce and the children met me in Minneapolis. Together we drove to Bozeman, Montana. At the same time our possessions were traveling by rail to Edmonton. No one was happy. It was October 1973, and it was the beginning of the worst time in our lives.

Joyce and the children stayed near Bozeman with her parents. Leonard (Joyce's brother) and I drove to Edmonton. The purpose was to find a place to live and unload the rail car. If we failed to unload the rail car within three days of arrival, the railway would impose a daily fee.

We were fortunate. My uncle, Sam Ardema, was a real estate agent in Edmonton. I had phoned him from Bozeman and told him what money we had. He realized that our only hope was to find subsidized housing. On arrival he showed us three possibilities. One was a relatively new three-bedroom townhouse in West Edmonton and I immediately took it. The next day Leonard and I moved our possessions from the train to the townhouse. We unpacked the beds, but little else. We had no way to secure the motorcycle, so it was parked inside. We then drove back to Bozeman.

The next day Joyce and I and the children set off for Edmonton. It had not occurred to either of us that some paper work should have been done in advance. When we arrived at the border crossing near Coutts, Alberta, the customs agent asked the usual questions. We told him we were moving to Edmonton and that our furniture was already there.

He asked for the appropriate papers. We had none. He looked at us in disbelief. He considered sending us back, until he looked in the back seat and saw the three children. He told us to meet him inside the customs office. He immediately set to work. He phoned his head office in Ottawa and asked them to remain available. Ottawa was two hours ahead and it was nearly closing time.

He filled in the documents as quickly as possible. He then phoned Ottawa and obtained verbal approval. By the time we left everything was approved, including family allowance. One month later we received our first check.

Whenever I think of our move, I thank God for three people: Leonard, my Uncle Sam and the customs agent. Late that evening we arrived at our new home, broke and unhappy, but relieved.

* * * * * *

Joyce's first priority was the children. She did everything she could to ensure that they felt secure and happy. Notwithstanding the upcoming difficulties, she was always a mother first.

The snow had come early and it was cold. We had only one vehicle and the bus stop was several blocks away. We had no close friends. Consequently, Joyce and the children were largely housebound. She would read to them, quiz them, teach them and stimulate their minds in whatever way she could. I believe that one of the reasons that all of our children continued their education can be attributed to Joyce's influence.

Joyce is very organized and efficient. During that time every dollar was spent to obtain the maximum benefit for the family. To assist, she used tokens, coupons and other specials. She also babysat two other children during the day while their mother worked.

To make some extra money both boys delivered a weekly local paper. Included in the paper were flyers and other promotional material. Many families wanted the papers, but asked that the flyers not be delivered. Before throwing them into the trash, Joyce would review them.

In one case a fast food chain offered hamburgers for 25 cents, if certain coupons were returned. We saved as many coupons as we could. When it was Vincent's birthday, we picked up 25 hamburgers for his party.

In another case, a local radio station, along with a downtown restaurant, offered free dinners to the family who predicted the temperature on the first day of spring. Joyce and the boys filled out all the available forms and returned them. We received coupons for six dinners to Mother Tucker's. The dinner was delicious.

My first priority was to find a job. My Uncle Sam had recommended that I consider real estate sales. It required very little capital. All that was required was that I pass a two-week course offered by the Real Estate Board. I agreed.

Unfortunately, the course was not offered until spring. I would have to find something in the meantime. I became a security guard at the Misericordia Hospital. My most important function was to be available to the staff in the emergency room to subdue drunks if necessary. There was significant down time. This enabled me to prepare to become a real estate agent.

Security guards are not paid in advance. We needed money immediately so I sold my motorcycle for $300. The person who bought it looked like an escaped felon. He was fully bearded and tattooed. He paid with cash pulled from his boot.

About two years after I sold my motorcycle, the doorbell rang. At the door was a police officer. "Where's your motorcycle?" he asked. I told him that I had sold it about two years before.

"Yes I know," he said, "and you did not pay the excise tax on it." He handed me an invoice from the Government of Canada for $290. "You have three months to pay it."

I had no idea what an excise tax was. He then explained that anything brought into the country is subject to an excise tax, if sold within two years of importation. Because I had sold it within the two years and because I had not paid the tax in a timely fashion, penalties had accrued. It all added up to almost what I received for the motorcycle.

Real Estate Sales

In early 1974 I began working as a real estate agent for Melton Real Estate. In the fall of that year we purchased our first home. The next winter, we received an invitation to attend a real estate sales presentation in Edmonton. We decided to attend. The real estate being offered was located on Padre Island, Texas. John and Diane Ludwig were also at the meeting. After the presentation we met with them. We all decided to accept the real estate company's offer to see the property. All costs for the three-day trip were on the company, including the cost of travel. The offer was available between Christmas and New Year's Day.

The company made all the arrangements. The plane was full of like-minded people. We landed in Corpus Christi and were shuttled to Padre Island. The next day the company drove us around to see the various properties and amenities. After the parade of properties, we met with some of the salespeople.

That day, the Ludwigs received word that their oldest daughter, Ann, had been murdered in Vancouver by her husband, Bruce Chester. Together they had a daughter, who was seventeen months old at that time.

Naturally, the Ludwigs were devastated. I cannot imagine worse news. Their grief was tangible. They spent much of the evening on the phone attempting to get additional information. Their primary concern was for their granddaughter. They wanted to go to Vancouver as quickly as possible.

Because the company had booked the flights, any changes had to be made by them. They immediately began to make arrangements to fly the Ludwigs to Vancouver. We spent the entire evening with them. Most of the time was spent walking on the beach. Eventually they received word that they would be departing the next day. We helped them pack. Thereafter, Diane was exhausted and went to bed.

John was ordinarily not an emotional or demonstrative person. But that night as he walked on the beach, he exposed his soul. He talked about his love for Ann, and how intelligent and gifted she was. He talked about how she had always confided in him. When she started dating Bruce, her attitude changed.

John disliked Bruce. He thought that Bruce was abusive and disrespectful of Ann. He could not understand why she stayed with him. She was clearly his intellectual superior and yet she allowed him to bully her. He had strongly advised her to leave him, which had resulted in a near violent confrontation with Bruce. He said he felt guilty for not having done more. Occasionally, we would just walk back and forth on the beach as he wept silently.

The longer he talked the more he expressed his

concern for his granddaughter. He loved her with the same intensity that he had loved Ann. He wanted nothing more than to take responsibility for her. That is what they intended to do upon arriving in Vancouver. He said it was his understanding that she was currently with Bruce's parents. Eventually at about 3 a.m. he went to his room.

The next day, they looked as though they had not slept at all. They left for Vancouver at about noon. A few days after we returned to Edmonton we learned that John and Diane were home with their granddaughter. They immediately retained a lawyer for purposes of adopting her. Because of their acrimonious relationship, Bruce refused to consent to the adoption.

John and Diane were members of the West End Christian Reformed Church. They wanted to baptize their granddaughter and they wanted me to conduct the service. I agreed. They also wanted special music. They called council and received permission to have me conduct the service, but council would not permit the special music. Apparently, their request for special music was denied because "the service was for worship, and not for performances."

I was angry. I had prepared a sermon on the various types of baptism referenced in the Bible. But that night as I fumed about what had happened, I prepared another sermon. The sermon was based on John 4:23: "Yet a time is coming and has now come when the true worshipers will worship the Father in spirit and truth, for they are the kind of worshipers the Father seeks" (New International Version).

I preached about how worship services had become scripted, i.e., that every worship service was the same as every other. There was the salutation, the long prayer, the collection, the sermon and the benediction. For some people the service was worship. Consequently, any change would be a violation of what they believed worship to be. And wasn't that simply a reversion to the hypocritical practices of the Pharisees? After each example was a sarcastic and recurring refrain. It was: "and God laughed." And so it went.

To this day I truly regret that sermon. It had been a complete misuse of Scripture. No one was edified by it. I later told John how much I regretted it, but I never did apologize to the congregation. I should have. Instead, I decided that if anyone ever complained to me about it, I would apologize to that person. No one ever did. Hopefully that meant that the sermon was just as ineffective as some of my previous sermons had been.

Thereafter John and Diane attended Bruce's trial. He was found guilty. At any trial the prosecutor is not required to prove motive. They must prove what happened, or how it happened, but not why it happened. As a result, when they attended the trial they learned what happened, but not why. John would often express his frustration in not knowing. One day he again spoke to me about it. He asked me if I knew of any way of finding out why Ann had been killed. I told him that as far as I knew, there were only two ways to find out: one was to ask the prosecutor, and the other was to ask Bruce.

He said that he had already asked the prosecutor but he had refused to say. He also knew that Bruce would never want to speak with him. He asked me if I would talk to Bruce. Although I was very reluctant, I found it impossible to say no. I had seen their suffering on Padre Island. I knew how important this was to them. I told him I would try.

I called the B.C. Penitentiary, which was a maximum-security prison in New Westminster B.C. I told them that I was a Chaplain with the Christian Reformed Church and that I wanted to visit Bruce Chester. They obtained some information from me and said that if Bruce agreed they would call me back. Within a few days they did call back. Bruce had agreed. I flew to Vancouver and prepared to meet with him.

The B.C. Penitentiary was a very old building. It was built in 1878, almost one hundred years earlier. When I arrived I told them who I was, and who it was that I wanted to see. I showed them my ministerial credentials. They ushered me in. The whole experience was somewhat disconcerting. The further I proceeded into the jail, the greater the number of doors that shut behind me.

I had expected a "glass" visit, i.e., a visit where two people sit opposite each other at a row of desks with an intervening glass partition. However, because I was a chaplain, I was given a "room" visit. There were no partitions, just the two of us. Bruce was already in the room when I arrived.

I introduced myself and we engaged in some small talk. I then told him that, as a chaplain, I was interested in knowing why people do the things they do. I asked him if he wanted to talk about it. He said "sure." What surprised me was that he was not in the least bit reluctant. He would often go on at length. If I asked for more detail, or history, he would provide it. It was surprisingly easy. His story was as follows.

His relationship with Ann had always been stormy. His relationship with her family was even worse. They had moved to Vancouver for a new start. It helped only in that her family wasn't there. Ann was riding him and they often argued. He smoked some dope and she resented it, especially after the baby was born. He had not wanted children. She was pushing him to get a regular job, but jobs were hard to come by.

The pregnancy seemed to change her. It got worse after the baby was born. Ann would often talk about leaving. Then one day it came to a head. She said she wanted their daughter baptized. He hated anything religious and definitely did not want her baptized. This was his child too. Shouldn't he also have some rights? She started packing. She said she was going back to Alberta. She was taking their daughter and she would have her baptized in Edmonton. The last straw was when she said that they would live with her parents.

He said that he was angry, frustrated and ignored and that he simply lost it. They started fighting. He admitted that he killed her and told me how he did it. He appeared to have no remorse. The conversation lasted about forty-five minutes. He seemed to want to talk more, especially about political matters, but I had what I wanted and left. I told John and Diane what I had learned. I believe it provided them some comfort. For John it provided some closure.

* * * * *

In the summer of 1975 I decided to take flying lessons. I justified it on the grounds that I could then show out-of-town properties from the air. The flight school was located at the Edmonton Municipal Airport. I was required to log about ten hours before I was permitted to fly solo. The first few hours were in the classroom, and the remaining hours were in the air. Although the flight school and aircraft were located at the Municipal

Airport, the actual in-air training was done at the small Villeneuve Airport, about fifteen miles northwest of Edmonton.

One day we were practicing "touch and go" at Villeneuve. This is a procedure whereby the pilot simply touches the runway, as if landing, but then powers up and goes. On the way back to the Municipal Airport, my instructor told me to land the plane.

Generally speaking, learning to fly is easy. The one thing I found difficult was understanding the radio. There was always static on the radio and it crackled all the time. The voice from the control tower was always broken. I would constantly ask them to repeat themselves, which did not please them. After receiving clearance to land, the static on the radio was particularly bad, so the instructor turned the radio off. I decided to take a long slow glide path back to the runway. This would be the perfect landing. Unknown to us, the control tower was trying to tell us to take a short glide path, because the airbus from Calgary was also about to land. Of course, we heard nothing.

Just as I was about to bring the plane down, the instructor turned the radio back on. The control tower was screaming at us. I couldn't understand much of what they said, but my instructor could. He immediately took control of the plane and flew it to the side of the runway. I think his intentions were to land the plane in the grass.

We were practicing in a Piper Cub airplane, which has a plastic bubble over the cockpit. I looked back. Not more than 200 yards behind us, the airbus, a Boeing 737, was attempting to land, but we were still in the way. Consequently, the pilot of the airbus was forced to abort his landing. He applied power. The sound, as he flew over us, was deafening. The force of the exhaust from the 737 hit the top of the Piper Cub, essentially planting us into the grass. The instructor powered up and taxied the plane to the terminal. When we arrived, a member of the Ministry of Transport was standing at the gate. He took the keys from the instructor and I never saw him again.

The following week I flew to Villeneuve with my new instructor. After some touch and goes, we decided to do a number of insipient spins. An insipient spin is what happens immediately after an airplane stalls in the sky. Because of the weight of the motor, the front end drops first and as it drops, the plane begins to spin. If the pilot allows the spin to continue, the result is a full spin. In either case the solution is to apply power and the plane essentially flies itself out of the spin.

After we had done a number of insipient spins, the new instructor asked me if I wanted to do a full spin. I said yes. He said he would do the first one and I would do the next. As it turned out, I never did the next one. We climbed to the appropriate altitude and he powered off. Eventually the front end fell and the plane began to spin in a corkscrew fashion straight for the ground.

What I had not anticipated was the effect the spinning motion would have. By the time he powered on I was already sick. Again we climbed to the appropriate altitude and he asked me if I wanted to take this one down. I said no, so he powered down, and the plane again corkscrewed itself downwards. At the last moment he powered back up. The result was that momentarily the plane was actually accelerating downward before turning back up. I tried not to look, but did anyway.

By this time I was thoroughly sick and began to retch. For the first time the instructor realized I was sick. He flew back as quickly as possible. We arrived at the terminal just in time. I went into the washroom and did what I had to do. The instructor came in twice to ask how I was doing. There was nothing he could do so I asked him to leave. After about 45 minutes I looked in the mirror. I was green. I drove home and went to bed where I remained for two days. My flying lessons were over.

* * * * *

From 1974 to 1976 the real estate market was very good. Agents were busy; the money was good. Nonetheless it was, in many ways the worst of times. Joyce was unhappy. She had loved supporting the ministry and had excelled in that role. She was admired and respected by all parishioners. She had many friends. Now she had no car. Transportation by bus was almost impossible, especially with three children. Under those circumstances it was difficult to make friends. She was often lonely and, given my work, she was often alone. She was far removed from her comfort zone. What she needed was reassurance. What she had was a husband blinded by his own need to succeed. In our second year, Joyce did some substitute teaching that helped.

I was also unhappy. I did not enjoy my work. I continued with it only because the money was good. It was a means to an end, but the end seemed distant. Our relationship was strained. The nature of the work contributed to our difficulties. My time was never my own. My company required a certain level of performance and clients required a certain level of service. Most purchasers worked during the day. Consequently most homes could only be shown in the evening. Many offers were also written and presented in the evening. Sometimes the negotiations continued well into the night. I was seldom home.

There was however, one thing that we agreed on. The children would always remain our top priority. In the spring of 1976, Chad was born. His birth was a godsend in many ways. He was a wonderful child. Joyce has always loved being a mother and Chad's birth provided her with a renewed purpose.

* * * * *

Although I was not particularly happy with my work, it did give me the opportunity to work with and appreciate Ben Vanden Brink. He was a lawyer in a large law firm in Edmonton whom I would often consult on various transactions. We would eventually practice law together.

In the summer of 1976, Ben Vanden Brink, Randall Neu (my doctor) and I decided to go on a motorcycle trip. I borrowed my brother's motorcycle. Randall has a very quick wit and an unrivaled capacity to paint word pictures. He can also impersonate almost anyone.

Just before we left we were on the parking lot of a mall in Red Deer. The purpose was to pick up some supplies for the trip. A lady was slowly backing out of a parking stall and in doing so she accidently bumped another lady who was walking behind her car. The pedestrian banged on the driver's side door, and the fray was on. The driver jumped out of her car and slapped the other. Both were screaming, cursing, slapping and pulling hair. We watched until it was over. "So much for the thin veneer of respectability," observed Randall.

The plan was to see the California redwoods and on the way back explore the town of Gold Beach, Oregon.

Randall was considering Gold Beach as a place to relocate his medical practice. We were to return home within two weeks. We also agreed that we would not pre-plan any day. We would simply travel until someone wanted to stop, and then proceed the next day. As it turned out, both Ben and Randall wanted to stop at every bar we passed. Because I drink very little, I would spend my time maintaining the bikes, finding accommodation for the night or simply having lunch.

We crossed the border near the Waterton Glacier International Peace Park. The border guard asked the appropriate questions: "Who are you?" and "What do you do?" To the question "What do you do?" he received the following answers: from Ben, "I am a lawyer," from Randall, "I am a doctor," and from me, "I am a preacher."

"Tell that to someone who believes it," he said as he picked up the phone. "Hey Charlie, I have some smart-ass bikers who claim to be a lawyer, a doctor and a preacher. I think you'd better check them out." He then sent us inside. When inside we spent about an hour convincing Charlie that we were who we said we were. In the meantime we could see through the window that other officers were checking out our bikes.

An hour later we were on our way. We traveled about ten miles to the small settlement of Robb, Montana, which is located in the middle of the Blackfeet Indian Reservation. It was there that Ben and Randall spotted the first bar, so we stopped.

We pulled into the parking lot that was already full. There were Native Americans everywhere. As soon as we stopped we were approached by a number of them.

"What are you doing here?" one demanded.

"We are here to have a drink," was the reply.

"What if your bike isn't here when you get out?" asked another as he staggered forward. He was clearly drunk.

"Then I will pay you to protect my bike," said Randall as he pulled out a ten- dollar bill, and gave it to the drunken man.

"Thanks, buddy," drawled the drunk as he sat on the motorcycle, gripping the handlebars tightly so as not to fall off. "Thanks."

With that we went in. The bar was full. The music was loud. People were dancing. The only space available was at the bar. Ben and Randall each ordered a beer. I ordered a coke.

Suddenly the music and the dancing stopped. Someone from the band came over to talk to us. "This is a private gathering," he said, "and you are not welcome here. You have to go now."

We didn't need a second invitation. We left. There was a small group hanging around our motorcycles. The drunken person was still sitting on Randall's bike and was still gripping the handlebars.

187

When Randall reached to take it, the drunk tried to backhand Randall across the face. "Some guy paid me to protect this bike," he slobbered, "and that's what I'm going to do." He gripped the handlebars even more tightly.

"He doesn't recognize you," I said.

Randall thought for a moment then whispered into the drunk's ear, "How much did the guy pay you?"

"Ten bucks," the drunk stammered.

"Ten bucks! Is that all?" Randall asked with a smirk. "Then why don't we steal it? This thing is worth more than ten bucks."

The drunk turned slowly. "That's a great idea," he slurred. Randall waited for him to get off but he continued to grip the handlebars.

"Then you have to get off," said Randall.

"Ya, I guess you're right," he laughed. He tried to un-straddle the motorcycle but when he did, he fell to the ground. It was our opportunity, and we were gone.

After traveling a number of days, we were only in Idaho. It was late one evening. Ben and Randall were in another bar and I had been outside attending to the motorcycles. When I walked in, I noticed the bar was full. It may have been payday. The bartender greeted me warmly. "I hear you're a preacher," he said, "and I hear you're a pretty good singer."

I looked at Ben and Randall. I realized that I was

being set up for something, but I didn't know what. "They tell me you will sing for us," the bartender continued, pointing to Ben and Randall.

"Maybe yes, maybe no," I answered, "but I need a coke first."

When I sat down, Ben and Randall gave me their story. Apparently, the music group scheduled for the evening had not shown up and the patrons were not happy. The bartender had asked Ben and Randall what they did for a living. They said that we were gospel-singers, and that I was the lead singer. The bartender had asked them if we would sing for his patrons. Ben asked what was in it for us. The bartender said he would pay us the same as he would have paid the other group. I cannot remember how much it was, but I think it was about fifty dollars per person. In addition, the food and drink would be on the house. Ben told him that he and Randall could not sing, because they already had too much to drink, but he thought I would because I seldom drank.

After I had the coke the bartender came back. "Will you sing for us?" he asked loudly enough for everyone to hear.

"Yes, sir," I replied, "but I won't sing alone. We are a group and we always sing together. So ask them." I pointed to Ben and Randall, who both looked as though they had just been double-crossed.

The bartender did ask them. They said no. Then the

bartender took the microphone and announced to the crowd that we were a gospel-singing group from Canada and would they like to hear us sing? "Yes," they shouted. The bartender looked at us. No one moved. "Louder," he barked, looking at the crowd. "Yes," the crowd screamed.

Over the noise Ben shouted into my ear, "What should we sing?"

"I don't care," I shouted back. "What songs do you know?"

"I think I know Amazing Grace," he replied.

We told the bartender that we would sing. To the cheers of the crowd we made our way to the stage. We had no music. We huddled.

"What the hell are we doing?" asked Randall quietly. "I don't know the words."

"Then just hum," Ben advised. "We're into it now."

It turned out that I was the only one who knew the words and the tune. Two words into the song and it was obvious that we were not harmonizing. It was also obvious that despite his best effort, Ben had forgotten the words. He was trying to get the words from me, and as a result he was a half note behind. He would catch up when there was a line he knew. In the meantime, Randall was humming a tune known only to himself.

People were looking at each other in disbelief. Some were laughing. About a third of the way through someone shouted, "Those guys can't sing. They sound like crap." By this time everyone was laughing, or hooting or waving their arms as if to say, "Get out of here." Ben and I stood there grinning sheepishly. Randall looked like he wanted to kill somebody.

The bartender came on stage and gave Ben and Randall their bills. "Pay your bills and get out of here," he snarled. In discussing this matter later, I pointed out that I was the only one who didn't have to pay for my drink.

A few days later we were somewhere in Nevada. We were on a curvy stretch of road where we decided to take some pictures. One of us would go up the road and around a curve. Then we would take pictures of the other two coming around the curve. Naturally, the higher the speed the greater the "lean" of the motorcycle as it came around the curve.

It was to be the last shot of the day. Randall and I were ahead waiting for Ben to round the curve but he was going too fast. He was not able to hold the road and slid to the bottom of a thirty-foot ravine. We thought he was dead. We ran back. By the time we got to the bottom of the ravine Ben was stirring. At first all we could hear was some groaning. Then Ben began to talk, albeit in very short sentences. Randall soon determined that nothing was broken, but Ben needed care. All the skin on his back had been scraped off.

One of the reasons it had taken so long to cross the

border was because Randall had taken a doctor's bag. In it he had all sorts of medications, including narcotic painkillers. Now was the time to use them.

We left Ben's motorcycle behind. Randall took Ben and I took the suitcases and we raced for the nearest town. We found a motel and Randall went to work. He first washed Ben's back with some scotch whiskey that Ben carried with him. The scotch not used on the back was used as a painkiller. Then he prepared a poultice that he smeared on Ben's back.

It was the most remarkable bit of doctoring I have ever seen. For three days and nights Ben lay face down. In the meantime Randall and I retrieved his motorcycle. When Randall cared for Ben, I cared for his bike. Three days later we were back on the road.

While we were on the motorcycle trip, Joyce had taken the children to Montana to stay with her parents. When it became clear that we would not be home within two weeks as planned, Joyce and I decided to meet at her sister's place near Seattle, Washington. She left the children in Montana and flew to Seattle. I flew in from Reno.

After the weekend with Joyce, I flew back to Reno to pick up my motorcycle. Ben and Randall had traveled on while I was gone, so I had some catching up to do. When I caught up with them, they seemed particularly happy to see me. I soon learned why. I was the only one with any money.

One of Randall's saddlebags was missing. It was the one that contained their money. They did not know whether it was stolen or had fallen off. They had gone back to look for it, but were not able to find it. They had made arrangements to have funds transferred to a bank in Sacramento but had insufficient funds to get there so they decided to wait for me.

Randall's motorcycle looked awkward with only one saddlebag, so somewhere on our way to Sacramento, he kicked the other one over a cliff. After they picked up the transferred funds, we decided to celebrate. We selected an elegant-looking restaurant. Once seated, Randall began to impersonate President Gerald Ford and Jimmy Carter, who was the democratic challenger at that time. He pretended that they were having a discussion on the merits of invading Mexico.

The owner of the restaurant could hear Randall. He asked if he could sit at our table. Ben and I were apprehensive, but we agreed and Randall carried on. Soon patrons encircled our table listening to Randall's impersonations. That evening all our food and drinks were on the house.

We had already been on the road for over two weeks. We had seen what we had come to see and it was now time to go home.

Returning home from our motorcycle trip

* * * * *

I believe that almost all parents of small children do whatever they can to protect their children from harm. The problem is that harm is occasionally difficult to identify and consequently children can be harmed despite their parent's best efforts.

In August 1976, Joyce and I took our children to Jasper National Park for a short vacation. While there we took a boat ride across Maligne Lake to a picnic area on an island in the middle of the lake. On the boat were a brother and sister from Edmonton. His last name was

Segal, and we believe that his first name was Alan but we are no longer sure. Both appeared to be in their thirties or forties.

The boat trip to the island was leisurely, and we had ample time to talk with the brother and sister. Both claimed to be professors at the University of Alberta. He taught psychology with a specialty in gifted children. He immediately took an interest in Vincent and Delbert who were seven and eight years old at the time. He was very friendly and engaged them in conversation whenever he could. He also took a number of pictures of the boys, including one of Del driving the boat. He kept telling us what wonderful boys we had and that as a psychologist he could see that they were very gifted. We were flattered.

When we arrived at the picnic area he invited the boys to go hiking with him. It was then that I began to feel disquieted. He had not invited me, so I said no. During the picnic he was as friendly as before. He played word games with the boys, but this time he included Joyce and I. Everything seemed entirely proper.

On the way back he again took a number of pictures. Both Joyce and I found him to be engaging. He was pleasant and cheerful. We exchanged phone numbers with him. By this time I wondered if my previous anxiety had been misplaced.

When Joyce and I were alone I told her about

195

Segal's invitation to the boys. She also thought that the invitation was inappropriate.

Approximately two weeks later Segal called. He said that he had the pictures developed and they had turned out well. He invited us to his home for a barbecue and to see the pictures. He made sure that we understood that the children were welcome.

We told him that we would get back to him. We both felt that his invitation to go hiking with the boys indicated that he was more interested in them than us. This made us uncomfortable. We called him back and declined the offer. We told him that we could not make the barbecue, and suggested that he send the pictures, which he did.

Shortly thereafter we received another call from him. He asked if we had received the pictures. He reminded us that he was a professor at the University and that he was working on a project for gifted children. He said that he was very impressed with our boys and would like to have them tested at the University. They would be tested one evening a week for six weeks. He would pick them up and return them.

Joyce and I discussed his invitation. Neither of us had reason to disbelieve him, yet both of us felt a certain level of discomfort. We said no.

We did not hear from him again, but we did hear about him. About a year later we read in the newspaper

196

that he had been charged and convicted of child sexual molestation.

* * * * *

Management

In September 1976, I became the manager of the Jasper Place Branch for Melton Real Estate. It was the same office where I had worked as a sales agent. Every weekday morning I chaired a sales meeting with all my agents. New listings were discussed and sales were noted. We would then travel from house to house to inspect the new listings. During the day I reviewed all offers and contracts. Once the contracts were finalized they became my responsibility. This was to enable the agents to concentrate on sales. A significant amount of my time was spent with mortgage companies and lawyers. A certain amount of time was also set aside to train the new recruits. Many evenings were spent assisting the newer agents in writing up and presenting offers. Negotiations would sometime extend well into the evening.

In addition to my daily obligations, I was responsible for retaining and recruiting my own sales staff. At that time, all my agents paid 50% of their income to the company. Of that 50%, half was retained by head office and my office retained the other half. From the money retained by my office, all expenses had to be paid. What was left after expenses was my income. As such, it was in my interest to recruit and retain the very best agents. In fact, 50% of my income was generated by 20% of the agents. All my efforts were directed at supporting the agents and making them more profitable. In our company, managers were not allowed to sell. Doing so would put us in conflict with the very agents that we were supposed to support.

Several of my agents had also applied for the position of manager. Many were unhappy, not because I became the manager but because they had not. Retaining them was my first priority. All of those who had competed against me were top producers and I could not afford to lose them.

Over time all those agents accepted my promotion, except for one. He was bitter and made no effort to hide it. For the sake of his children I will call him Dick, although that was not his real name. At that time he was married with three children. It did not help that prior to my promotion we did not like each other. We had often exchanged unpleasant words. A year or two before my appointment, several of the younger male agents from our office decided to go to Las Vegas for a weekend. At first we kept the trip a secret from Dick but eventually he found out and to our dismay, he insisted on coming along.

While we were in Vegas, I learned how uncouth and vulgar he actually was. We were all having dinner together. He ordered chicken. After eating most of the meal with his fingers, he began to eat the bones. What made it worse was that he always ate with his mouth open. The sight and especially the sounds were disgusting. He was also a heavy drinker and at dinner he had a number of hard drinks.

After dinner we decided to walk the strip. For most of us the shows were too expensive. We were barely out of the restaurant and Dick began to retch. He then stumbled over to an open convertible and puked on the front seat. Some in our group, including myself, told him that what he had done was disgraceful. He thought it was funny.

Later that same evening we were all in one room, playing cards. Each game cost the participant one dollar. He was losing, but not much. Suddenly he got up. "If I'm losing money anyway," he said, "I may as well get laid." With that he walked to the phone and called an escort agency. He then continued to play cards. Soon there was a knock on the door. It was his escort and they left to go to his room.

About an hour later, there was another knock on the door. It was Dick and his escort. He wondered if any of us would be interested in her. He began to tell us what she had done for him and how good she was. I had enough. I told him that even if I were interested I wouldn't want seconds after his filthy hands had touched her.

Then Bob, (one of my friends who had organized the trip) joined in. He had even more choice words for Dick. The escort left, but the shouting and the name calling continued. Bob told Dick that we had never wanted him on the trip in the first place. That was why we had kept it a secret from him. Finally, we all went to our respective rooms.

Now I was Dick's manager. I knew that I would either have to fire him or try to reconcile. I decided on the latter. I suggested to him that he and I go trout fishing in British Columbia for a weekend. I told him I would pay. He agreed. All weekend I attempted to talk to him. I learned that he was not an introspective person. He could not understand why some of us didn't like him. He often brought up the Vegas incident. He could not understand why we were angry with him – he was only trying to help.

Although I wanted him to talk, I had no interest in fighting old wars, especially given that he appeared to have no capacity for self-analysis. When I asked him if he thought that puking in the convertible was appropriate he seemed confused. To him it was just a joke, and he couldn't understand why we were upset by it. He hadn't hurt any of us.

I asked him if he had anything against me. He said no, but then went on about how I had treated him in Vegas. I asked him if he was hurt when he was not initially invited to Vegas. Again he said no. I told him that if he were hurt, then I would be prepared to apologize. "What for?" he asked. Eventually I gave up, and tried to enjoy the fishing.

Although our relationship was never good, it was at least better than before the weekend. We tolerated each other. Years later I received a call from a friend of mine who was a manager for the same company. He told me that Dick had been murdered in his own home by a prostitute.

* * * * *

Given the financial structure of the company, recruiting new agents was not difficult. In the first three or four months after an agent was hired, they often made nothing. Even if they had made a sale on the first day, they were not paid until after the possession date. Because they made nothing during that period, they paid the company nothing.

Retaining productive agents was another matter. There were a number of other real estate companies that charged a monthly fixed fee of approximately $1500, which was payable whether the agents made any money or not. Basically the agents paid for office space, some clerical support and supplies. These companies provided little or no sales support to the agents. However, for established and experienced agents, such support was no longer necessary and there was a financial advantage in joining the competition.

At that time a successful agent was anyone who made $50,000 or more per year. If he worked for us, he would pay $25,000 to the company, leaving him $25,000 as his annual income. If he joined the competition he could make $32,000 per year ($50,000 - $18,000 = $32,000). The net effect was, that from a financial point of view, our company was an attractive workplace for new recruits and moderately successful agents. For highly productive agents the competition was often more attractive.

We did, however, have one advantage. Our company had an excellent reputation. It was locally owned and it supported many worthwhile causes. Consequently, many people would call only our company when they wished to sell. Those calls were precious.

Every agent was given "floor time." This meant that they were the beneficiaries of whatever calls came in while they were in the office. For some agents, it was the principle source of their income. In other companies floor time was not nearly as profitable.

In the final analysis however, whether an agent stayed or left depended on the relationship he had with his manager. The manager was required to do whatever was necessary to keep him happy. This meant stoking his ego through verbal affirmation, awards, gifts, and various other perks such as trips and parties.

None of my agents left for financial reasons, but one left for other reasons. His wife was a painter and she donated one of her paintings to our office. Without consulting her, I hung the painting in the conference room. She was offended. She thought it should have been displayed in the entryway. I agreed, but the damage was done. She convinced her husband to go elsewhere.

In spite of the challenges, most of the agents were loyal and I enjoyed working with them. As previously indicated, recruiting new agents was not difficult. Training them, however, was time consuming. It was impossible to tell in advance who would become successful so it was essentially trial and error. Those who were not successful were eventually dismissed but in the meantime they had used up a great deal of my time and energy.

In Alberta the real estate market was robust. In other parts of the country it appeared to be less so. It occurred to me that there might be some agents with a proven track record who would consider a transfer to Alberta. To hire experienced agents would save me a great deal of time and effort. I advertised in the Toronto Sun. The ad stated that if they were chosen, I would pay their moving expenses. I received approximately ten responses. On a prearranged weekend, Joyce and I flew to Toronto and I interviewed all the respondents. Of those, I chose two. Both were married. One had two children.

The agent with the two children did reasonably well. He worked hard and I liked him. The other was a free loader. When he arrived in Alberta at my expense, he didn't even get his real estate license. Rather he applied for a different job altogether.

I did somewhat better when I recruited in Vancouver. I chose one agent, albeit with some reservations. He had a good but not exceptional track record and his motive for moving was unclear. Nonetheless he was charming, articulate and educated. He was also Pakistani, which I believed would be helpful. I decided to take a chance on him and he became one of my best agents.

* * * * *

Although I was very busy, I always tried to make time for my family. In the summer of 1977, Ben and his wife Sylvia gave us their older tent trailer, which they were no longer using. We were happy to have it. Attached to the hitch of the trailer was a jack. It was the type of jack that extended below the hitch.

My brother Andrew and his wife, Alice, also had a tent trailer. Our two families, along with some other friends, decided to go camping on a lake near Kelowna, B.C. The stay at the lake was enjoyable but when we left the campground, the jack became lodged between the two rails of a railroad track. The jack could not be removed because it had been welded on.

It appeared to us that our only option was to lift the rear of the trailer sufficiently high to allow the jack on the hitch to cross over the rail. Most of the people were enjoying the predicament I found myself in, especially my brother Andrew. Then we heard a train whistle but we could not see the train because of a curve in the tracks. The whistle sounded again, much closer. The family got out of the car and went up the road. Now, everyone was concerned, even Andrew.

There was no time to lift the rear of the trailer. I would simply have to try to pull the trailer over the rails. I backed up until the jack contacted the far rail. I put the car into low gear and stepped on the accelerator.

The trailer bounced violently upward but it was still lodged between the rails. The jack was acting as a lever, forcing the rear of the trailer up. Some one was shouting for me to run. That was, of course, my plan B. I got out of the car and looked at the jack. I noticed that the force of the first impact had bent the jack backward. As such it would require less height to get over the rail. I could hear the train approaching even without the whistle. I had one more chance.

I took another run at the rail. The rear of the trailer again shot upward, but this time the trailer bounced over the rail. It was dislodged. I was worried that the rail may have been bent, resulting in a train wreck, but there was nothing I could do. There wasn't even time to look at the track. In any event, there appeared to be no damage as the train sped noisily by.

I'm not sure if the violence on the railway tracks had anything to do with it, but several years later the tent trailer fell apart. We were on our way home from Thunder Lake, near Barrhead, Alberta. Suddenly, a car passed us. The occupant in the passenger seat was screaming for us to stop and pointing at the tent trailer. I looked in the rearview mirror. I could see nothing. I thought that we had lost the trailer. As I was slowing down, I saw smoke rising from where the trailer should have been.

After we stopped, I saw that we were still pulling the trailer, but it no longer had any wheels. They had peeled out from underneath and we had simply been dragging what was left along the road. The friction had created such heat that the entire bottom side was smoking. Unknown to us, pieces of the undercarriage had been breaking off as we were traveling. They were so hot they started fires in the dry grass along the highway. We were able to put out one fire close to where we had stopped. Other motorists were trying to put out other fires.

What made matters worse was the propane tank attached to the top of the hitch. It felt hot. I tried to remove it but it was bolted on. We disconnected the trailer, which was difficult enough given that the trailer and the car were no longer aligned. We were able to open the side door of the trailer and took out some belongings and left, leaving the trailer behind.

About five miles up the road we spotted an automobile salvage yard, and turned in. Old stripped-down cars were stacked on top of each other. We asked them if they would take the trailer and they said yes. We signed a bill of sale for one dollar and carried on.

* * * * *

For me the promotion to management was helpful. I could see that if things continued to go well, law school was possible. In many ways things did go well. In September 1977, we moved into a beautiful home in Westridge (an upscale district of Edmonton) on a quiet cul-de-sac. It had a very large backyard adjacent to a ravine.

We immediately installed a swimming pool. It was an investment we never regretted. All our children learned to swim. In the summers they enjoyed nothing more than to be at the pool with their friends. It was Del's responsibility to maintain the pool and Vince's responsibility to maintain the yard.

There were some significant disadvantages with the promotion. The demand on my time was even greater. My office accommodated about fifteen sales people. The turnover in real estate salespeople is always high and I was required to hire and train my own agents. I assisted them in preparing and presenting all offers for as long as they felt necessary. After the negotiations, many agents wanted nothing more than to have a drink with their manager.

Although Joyce and I both had a new focus, the new circumstances added new pressures to our relationship. Many of the agents loved to party and the previous manager had often held staff parties in his home. The same was expected of us. I drank very little, but some of my agents drank a lot. For them a party was nothing more than an excuse to drink as much as possible at someone else's expense.

Joyce resisted. She had seen enough drunken and vulgar behavior at previous parties. She did not want our home used as a venue for such unwholesome behavior. I insisted that not using our home was not an option – it was expected. She reluctantly agreed but by the time it was over, she promised herself never to host another "party."

The party went much as expected. By late evening several agents were drunk. One fell backwards while sitting on his chair. Dick vomited in the bathroom; most of it was on the floor. Another was smoking dope. About midnight they decided to go swimming. Someone organized a race. The non-participants would form the lanes and the contestants would swim two laps. The first to touch was the winner. Everyone wanted to challenge the manager. As such, I swam more than most. However, I had an advantage. I was sober. In one race, a contestant's girlfriend was part of the line that formed the lane. When I swam by, she tried to pull my swimming trunks down. By that time Joyce was thoroughly disgusted and angry. When the girlfriend came out of the pool, Joyce slapped her.

Nonetheless, we did have another party. This time, however, we had some friends that acted as bartenders. They were to monitor the amount the agents drank. It did not help much because the usual drinkers went to their vehicles to drink and by late evening they were drunk.

We decided to try something different. We would hold dinner parties every three months to acknowledge the top producers. We tried twice, but other agents crashed the parties and they were generally drunk by the time they arrived.

Joyce tried to be gracious and accepting, but it was difficult. She disliked most of the agents, their lifestyle, their values, and their behavior. She did not like that I was absent almost every evening. She did not want her home used as a venue for drinking. I told her that the only reason we had a home was because of the work of the agents. She felt that I was dismissive of her concerns and had lost my principles. I felt that she was unsupportive. We argued constantly. We had different goals and different values.

Our personalities did not mesh well in our new circumstances. I am goal-driven, impatient, impulsive and quick to anger. Joyce is value-driven, careful, cautious and conservative. One night I had had enough. We were into a full-throated argument. On impulse I decided to leave. I was angry and determined. I packed quickly and went to the car and found Joyce in the passenger seat.

"Where are you going?" I asked angrily.

"I don't know," she answered, "but I'm going wherever you go."

She refused to get out of the car. Then for the first time in many months we had a discussion as opposed to an argument. It wasn't as if we agreed, rather it was that we understood.

I saw something in Joyce that I very much admired

and respected. She was no happier with me than I was with her. Nevertheless, she was prepared to swallow her anger for what she believed was in the children's best interests. I admired the way she fought for what she believed. In my mind it was Joyce's finest hour. It was also the changing point in our relationship. We still argued, but never again did I consider leaving – not even on impulse. We tried harder to see issues from the point of view of the other.

There was another factor that changed my attitude. Often we don't appreciate what we have until we almost lose it. Although I was seldom home, when I was, I truly enjoyed my children. I realized that I would be desperately unhappy without them.

During this period I would occasionally go hunting on the farm on which I grew up. Sometimes I would take the boys, but on this occasion (which was shortly after I almost left Joyce) I went alone. I had decided to go goose hunting.

I had not hunted geese since the time on the lake and I had forgotten how traumatic it was. By this time I had learned that geese are absolutely committed to each other for as long as their mate is alive.

That day I shot another goose. The flock out of which this goose was a member flew on, but its mate did not. Rather it circled high overhead mournfully honking for its dead companion. This continued all afternoon.

211

Once before I had heard such a sorrowful sound. I thought about the goose that I had injured many years earlier. I wondered what had happened to that pair. I assumed that its partner had remained until the injured goose had died.

Then I began to weep. I thought about how committed these geese were to each other and about what an example they were to me. The affection, concern and commitment these geese demonstrated had shamed me. For a lack of commitment I had almost lost what I cherished the most—my family. I had never felt so disconsolate. That night the nightmares returned.

The next morning I returned to the place where I had shot the goose. There on the ground, exactly where the dead goose had fallen was its mate. When it saw me it flew away. But I then made a promise; I would never again harm one of those wonderful creatures from whom I had so much to learn.

* * * * *

Except for Dick, I liked and enjoyed my agents. There were some whose personality changed when they were drunk, but usually they were pleasant and cooperative. They worked hard and most were reasonably successful. In their private lives, however, many had issues.

One of the female agents was trying to become

financially independent so she could leave her husband. She was a minister's wife. She said that she had never loved her husband but had remained in the marriage for the sake of the children. Their children were adults now and as soon as she was financially independent, she planned to tell her husband that she was leaving. She said she was looking forward to telling him. In her view, he was nothing more than a sanctimonious asshole.

More often than not, many of the issues arose out of the misuse of alcohol or drugs. One of the male agents was married. His name was Jason and his wife was Jane. They had two beautiful daughters. The oldest could not have been more than six years old. It was clear that the marriage was strained. Although I do not know what the specific issues were, I do know that Jason drank far too much. He liked nothing more than to spend an entire evening in the bar. I have often wondered whether things may have turned out differently if he had spent those evenings at home.

Jason had all the listings from a particular home-builder. The builder's name was Frank and he was Jason's best friend. Jason worked hard for his friend and as a result both were doing well. Then one day Jane informed Jason that she and Frank had a longstanding sexual relationship. Jason was devastated. Shortly after he learned of the affair he died. He parked his car in the garage, closed the garage door, turned up the music on the radio, and kept the car running. He died of carbon monoxide poisoning.

At a subsequent morning meeting the agents talked about Jason's death. After the meeting two female agents approached me. Jason had told them that he was depressed and wanted to die. He also told them that he had life insurance payable to Jane, but only if the death was accidental. She would get nothing if his death were considered a suicide. He was angry with his wife but loved his daughters.

Both female agents felt terrible; neither had taken him seriously. One agent felt particularly guilty. She had been close to Jason and they often went to the bar together. An investigator from the life insurance company had contacted a number of my agents, but these two were the only ones that knew anything. He wanted to talk to them about Jason's death. They asked me what I thought they should do. I phoned Ben and asked whether my agents were required to talk to the investigator. He said no. I thought about the little girls left behind. I informed them that they were not compelled to speak to the investigator. In my view they would only contribute to the suffering if they talked. The little girls had done nothing wrong. They should not be made to pay for the sins of the parents. They agreed.

I later learned that the insurance monies were paid to the wife. I also learned that the affair between

Frank and Jane was over. Jane had told Jason about the affair because she wanted a divorce so as to marry Frank. However, Frank had no intention of leaving his wife. He had enjoyed Jane as a lover, but as a wife she was not an option.

After Jason learned of his wife's infidelity, he had spoken to Frank's wife. She was as shocked as Jason had been. For several months thereafter Frank and his wife attempted to make amends, but to no avail. They eventually divorced. I was told that both Frank and Jane remarried, but not to each other. Jane allegedly told one of her friends that there was no one she hated more than Frank.

I am not sure whether, as a group, real estate agents are less happy with their marriages than members of any other group. But I do believe that the nature of the work contributes to marital stress. The evening hours an agent is required to work conflicts with family life. But there is another factor that I believe destroys even more marriages, and that is the excessive use of alcohol. I make no judgment in respect to people who drink, but having observed the behavior of people such as Jason and especially Dick, I wish to say something about the drink itself.

Alcohol changes people. They do things they wouldn't otherwise do. They often make fools of themselves. Their judgment is impaired and their standards of conduct are lowered. They often become reckless.

Inhibitions are discarded. Alcohol robs people of opportunities. Companies do not hire or promote people who demonstrate that they cannot control their drinking. I was told that one of the reasons I was chosen to become the manager of the real estate office was because my superiors had never seen me drunk.

For some people alcohol may be addictive, for others it's a crutch. Either way, alcohol has ruined many lives, including Jason's. He was a good person. If he found it necessary to drink, I wish he had done it at home. Had he done so, his marriage might have survived and he might still be alive today.

* * * * *

In 1978 the Commonwealth Games were held in Edmonton. For some reason I wanted to meet with Ben, but I no longer remember why. In any event I learned that he was in a room at the Westin Hotel and he invited me to see him there. Queen Elizabeth was in Edmonton for the games and she was staying at the same hotel.

When I arrived, one of the elevators had been roped off for the exclusive use of the Queen. The elevator next to it was for the pubic. I pressed the up button. When the door opened, I stepped forward just as the Queen stepped out. We were within inches. A security person came from behind the Queen and pushed me aside. Nothing was said. He looked at the roped-off elevator, then he looked at me. I could see that he knew that they were on the wrong elevator.

After the games were over, I told two of my sales staff about my near encounter with the Queen. One of the agents had a British friend with her whose name was Ann. "I've always wanted to talk to the Queen," she said. "Why don't we call her?" She continued to push the idea, so we began to discuss various scenarios. We assumed that the Queen doesn't speak to just anyone so we knew we would need an angle. We finally narrowed our options to three.

1. I could call to apologize for almost bumping into her. We knew that I didn't have anything to apologize for, but that wasn't the point. We only wanted Ann to be able to say that she had spoken with the Queen on the speakerphone.

2. We could call to get the Queen's reaction to their mistake in taking the wrong elevator.

3. We could tell the Queen that we intended to go public with the story and we were calling to get her side of what happened.

None of the options were good, but we talked

ourselves into believing that there was at least a small chance. So we called information and asked to be put through to Buckingham Palace.

"Buckingham Palace," came the response. "How can I help you?" We had not expected any response and we were not ready.

"We would like to speak to the Queen," Ann stammered.

"Who shall I say 'we' are?"

"Ann."

"And what do you wish to discuss with Her Majesty?"

Ann looked at me, but I just shrugged my shoulders. This was her thing.

"My friend almost bumped into her and he wants to apologize," she said.

She was then asked about the details, which she provided. "Is your friend there?" asked the voice.

Now it was my turn. "Yes sir, I am here and I wish to apologize."

"I will transfer you," said the voice.

Soon another voice came on, and we went through the whole story again, except that this time I did all the talking. Ann could barely contain herself. She kept putting her hand over her mouth. Once she got up and did a short dance. Then we were transferred again. I believe it was to the Queen's secretary but I am no longer sure.

Once again we went through the whole story. He asked many questions. Then he said, "I will see if Her Majesty is available." Ann jumped out of her chair. We were all breathless. We waited. No one said anything. We just looked at each other in disbelief. I think we were all a bit afraid of what we were getting ourselves into.

Then the secretary came back on the phone. On behalf of Her Majesty, he thanked us for calling but she was not available. However, he would convey our apology.

* * * * *

Throughout the 1970's the real estate market was hot, fuelled by inflation. Prices were increasing by the month. People wanted to buy while they still could. At the same time, the value of money was decreasing. A dollar could not buy as much as it had a year earlier. From 1973 through 1982 the average annual rate of inflation was 8.74%. It reached its peak in 1980 at 13.58%.

In 1976, on the advice of our accountant, we began investing in property. The first properties purchased were Multi-Unit-Residential Buildings (MURBS). Why we purchased these MURBS requires some explanation. Throughout the 1970's real estate prices were increasing at an alarming rate. Because everyone was buying, there were few homes available, which of course drove the prices up.

The government believed that if they could increase the number of residential units, the prices would at least stabilize. Consequently, in about 1973 they changed the tax code. The change enabled wage earners to deduct from their taxable income the builder's entire start-up costs for MURBS. Once built, the title of the unit would be transferred to the wage earner. The start-up costs would often exceed the down payment.

Prices did not stabilize; they continued to escalate so we purchased a number of rental houses as well. The down payment was generally between 10 to 20%. The rent made the mortgage payments. We also purchased a 20-acre parcel of waterfront land at Buck Lake. After we obtained subdivision approval for approximately twenty lots, we built an access road. Sales were to begin in September 1979.

There were essentially three reasons why, by 1979, all of our savings were invested in real estate:

1. For tax reasons the MURBS had been rec-ommended by our accountant;

2. The houses and lakefront property were purchased to take advantage of the rising prices; and

3. I knew that financially we were getting close
    to the time that I could go to law school.
    Once there, I did not want to work. Classes
    would be difficult enough. The intent was to
    sell the properties while I was in law school.

During most of the six years that I was in real estate
Joyce was unhappy. Much of her unhappiness arose out
of the long hours that I worked. When we were first
married we shared a common goal. Together we would
raise a family and together we would do church ministry. From her point of view we were achieving neither of
these goals. Sadly, the church ministry was already lost.
In respect to the family, she felt that she could just as
well be a single mom. She thought that my first obligation was to be a full-time dad, and I was failing.

From my point of view, I thought I was the best
dad I could be under the circumstances. It was true that I
worked long hours, but when I was home I tried to spend
as much time with the family as possible. Even while at
work I tried to include them. When I went to Vancouver
to recruit agents, I took Del and Vince with me. I also
had an obligation to provide for the family, and always
there was the goal of self-sufficiency by the time I went
to law school.

What made matters worse was that it was getting
increasingly difficult to continue to manage both a real
estate office and our growing inventory of properties.

Our rental homes were profitable only if they were rented. Unfortunately, some of the tenants would leave the home in shambles when they left. More and more of my time was spent dealing with tenants and their concerns. In addition to my other obligations I was becoming a property manager. This exacerbated the problems at home.

Over time I realized that Joyce was right. Our children were eleven, ten, six and three years old. They needed more than a weekend dad. Therefore, in the fall of 1979, I resigned as manager of the real estate office so as to dedicate all my time to our family and to our real estate holdings. Our plan was to retain our rental homes from which we would receive some income and to spend as much time as necessary to sell the lake front lots. This would enable us to build up sufficient equity to permit me to go to law school. It would also make it possible to spend more time at home. Real estate values continued to rise and for a few short months it appeared that my decision to resign was prudent.

Unfortunately, our best-laid plans were not to be. The existing government programs had neither curtailed the rising price of real estate nor slowed the rate of inflation. Consequently in the latter part of 1979 the government substantially increased the prime lending rate and announced that they would continue to increase interest rates until prices stabilized. In 1981 interest rates rose to 21%. The result was that the real estate market collapsed. Everyone was trying to unload. The only way to sell in a collapsing market is to price the property below market value.

In a falling market it is important not to add to the cost of the property that you are trying to sell. As a result, it was during this time that I taught myself everything necessary to renovate a home. I learned how to roof, wire, plumb, drywall and install carpet or hardwood -- anything to make the property more attractive to a potential purchaser. I was now working harder than ever simply to minimize our losses. Because of the government's announcement the value of all real estate continued to spiral downward. Watching the equity in our properties disappear on a daily basis was stressful for both of us. For me the prospect of a career in law was diminishing.

The first casualties were the MURBS. In early 1980 the high interest rates caused the builder to declare bankruptcy. We never did get title to the property and the down payment was lost.

The second casualties were the lakefront lots. Notwithstanding our best efforts, not one lot sold. Only the property taxes continued.

The third casualties were the rental homes. We had purchased most homes by assuming the existing mortgage. The interest rates on these existing mortgages may have averaged 6% and most of the mortgages had a five-year term. However, by the time we purchased them, there may have been only one or two years left. When the term came due the current rate would apply. This meant that within a few years interest rates could increase from 6 to 21%. This doubled or tripled the mortgage payments.

Despite our financial difficulties, in 1980 I applied to various law schools for the 1981-82 school-year. One requirement of every law school is that the applicant take the Law School Admission Test (LSAT). Most law schools base their admissions on the results of these exams. In 1980 the LSAT was, I believe, based on 800 points and most law schools would accept all students who scored above 600 points.

When I wrote the LSAT I was surprised, not by how difficult it was, but rather by how little time I had for each segment. I am a relatively slow reader to begin with, and after the first two segments I had answered about half the questions. I tried to speed up but by the end of the three hour exam I had not completed a single segment. After approximately two months I was notified of my score. I cannot remember precisely what it was but I think it was just over 500 points. By the time I received my score it was too late to redo the exam. As expected, I was not accepted by any law school.

It was when I wrote my LSAT that I learned from

other students that it was possible to purchase tutorials that would help in writing the LSAT. Many of those writing the LSAT had done just that. The tutorials were essentially exams that had been used in the past.

After I learned that I was not accepted by any law school, I decided to try once more. This time however, I purchased a number of tutorials. For months I spent as much time as I could writing these exams. I tried to abide by the time allotted. In 1981 I wrote my second LSAT. This time my score was I believe, above 650 points and I knew that my chances for acceptance were good but not certain.

By this time our financial situation was near hopeless. Real estate was not selling well and we had very little income. I could go back to selling real estate but that was not an attractive option. I did not particularly like selling and if I did go back I would be absent much of the time and would again bear the weight of Joyce's disapproval.

Nonetheless, it was important that I have a job in the event I was not accepted. I applied for two positions that would be available at about the time I would know whether I was accepted or not. The first position was as a chief administrative officer for a town near Edmonton. The second position was with the Edmonton Real Estate Board. The entire process was a bit of a balancing act. I didn't want to commit to either position as long as law school was a possibility. However, given that our finances were a mess, I wanted to start work as soon as I learned that I was not accepted.

In the spring of 1982 I learned that I had been accepted into law school. By that time we had no income and all of our savings were lost. All we had left was one rental property and a little equity in our Westridge home. However, I did not want to be denied. By the time I enrolled I would be thirty-nine years old and another opportunity was not likely. The first thing I did was notify the town and the real estate board that I was no longer available. The next thing was to apply for the largest student loan possible. We had no trouble meeting the minimum requirements. Once again we started another phase of our life with no money. It would be the third time. The first time was the ministry; the second was real estate; and now law.

CHAPTER 8
LAW

Law School

In September 1982 I enrolled at the University of Alberta Law School. At the same time, Chad, our youngest son, started grade one, which enabled Joyce to work outside the home. Almost immediately she found a night job working for a food distribution company. When she came home in the morning she would prepare breakfast for the family. She slept when she could. When the children came home from school, she was always there for them and would go to work after they were put to bed.

The work was tedious and uninspiring. She prepared invoices for all the goods shipped to the various

227

grocery stores. The office was always filled with smoke. Her co-worker was an unhappy, opinionated older woman. In the winter the warehouse was always cold. When she returned home she was exhausted.

Financially, the years I spent in law school were difficult. However, from the point of view of our relationship it was the beginning of recovery. Joyce was doing everything she could to see me through. We were once again pulling in the same direction. I was happier than I had been in years. My childhood dream was within sight.

The first year was particularly difficult. The volume of material was overwhelming. I am not entirely sure, but I believe that all first year students were required to take five courses. Each day we attended three or four lectures. Each professor would issue reading assignments. The assignments generally required reading case law and many of the cases were twenty or thirty pages long. Try as I might, I was always behind.

Approximately half way through my first year, I asked a classmate how he was able to keep up. He said he couldn't and he thought no one could. All the students he knew studied in groups of three to five students.

In each group, one student would be assigned one or two courses depending on the number in the group. That student would then prepare a summary (called a "can"). On weekends the group would get together and exchange and review the various cans. Thereafter, I tried to find someone to study with, but most people already belonged to a group. None were prepared to share their cans with anyone outside the group.

In any event, after the first year I found myself in the bottom 10%. Several students were dismissed outright. Others were given an interview. Of those interviewed, an older Chinese student and I were given the opportunity to repeat the first year. I was disappointed, but not devastated. I knew I could do better. Of the five courses, I had failed only one. In the meantime, I had learned to study. I would form a group and try again.

There was also some good news. In April, about the time of my final exams, we received an offer on our home in Westridge, which we accepted. The possession date was for August 1. Although there was not much equity left, there was some. After real estate and legal fees were paid, we eventually netted about $9,000. The intent was to use the money only when absolutely necessary. Joyce needed no further encouragement to quit her job. She immediately gave notice.

We had one rental home left in Meadowlark (a lower-middle class district in Edmonton) and gave the tenants notice. There was a reason why the Meadowlark home was the only one left in inventory – the entire interior had to be renovated. We used the summer for that purpose and also built a garage. By August both the house and the garage were ready.

We all crowded into the Meadowlark home. The boys all slept in a room in the basement; Laura had a room upstairs. Space was limited. By Westridge standards, the home was modest. Nevertheless, neither Joyce nor any of the children ever complained.

The neighborhood was different and we found it inhospitable. It was a neighborhood in transition. People were always moving in and out. Except for the closest neighbor, it was difficult to make friends but it was where we lived and we all made the best of it.

On one occasion a neighborhood gang attacked Chad. On another occasion our home was broken into and some valuables were stolen. Thereafter we acquired a dog, which was helpful. Not long thereafter the dog began to bark furiously. It was approximately 1 a.m. I rushed to the window and saw several young people running down the driveway. The damage to the garage door indicated that they had been attempting to break into the garage.

Shortly after we moved, I found a job as a security guard at a nearby mall. I worked from 10 p.m. to 6 a.m., which corresponded to the time that the mall was closed. For eight hours I was the only one in the mall. My job was to lockup at 10 p.m., patrol the hallway and the sunken boiler room throughout the night, and open for the staff at 6 a.m. Within a few days the job had become painfully boring. Nothing ever happened. I tried to make it more interesting. For example, I included the flat roof as part of the patrol. The mall was only one storey high. The people on the parking lot did not expect that there would be someone on the roof. Consequently, they would not curtail their conversations or activities.

I also tried to make it more interesting by doing the patrol on bicycle. However, that did not last long. Someone saw me bicycling on the roof and called the police. Several police vehicles converged on the mall.

I began to make only periodic visits during the night. Eventually, I discontinued even those visits. Then something did happen. A pipe burst in the boiler room, apparently just after lockup. By the time I arrived at 6 a.m. the sunken boiler room was flooded to the top. Everything in the room was submerged. I was fired that day. I had been there for less than one month.

My next job was as a prison guard. It was perfect. The hours were flexible. While in law school I could work part-time and during the summers, full-time. During my repeat year at law school I worked part-time at the medium security jail in Fort Saskatchewan, Alberta, doing two night shifts every weekend. The jail was where the last hanging took place in Alberta and the hang-room was still there.

Although it was more dangerous, I preferred to work inside. It gave me the opportunity to do some studying. My outside responsibilities were to patrol the grounds with a four-wheel drive truck.

Depending on the traffic and the time, the jail was about one hour from home, which meant that every weekend I wasted four hours in travel time. Consequently, I asked for a transfer to the Edmonton Remand Center. It was granted and I continued to work there as long as I was in law school.

The remand center is the place where those who are arrested are held until their first appearance in court. If bail is not granted or cannot be met, the prisoner remains until trial. I enjoyed working at both the jail and the remand center. There was always an element of unpredictability, especially at the remand center. The prisoners in jail had all been convicted and some had been there for some time. They knew the routine. On many wards, they essentially governed themselves.

The prisoners in the remand centre, however, were more volatile. They were new to each other and the pecking order was always changing. As a result there were more fights. They were also new to the guards. We never knew what would set them off so we had to be more careful.

That fall Joyce found a part-time job working as a librarian for the Edmonton Christian School. It was work much better suited to her and she enjoyed it. She continued to work there until she moved to Red Deer.

In the fall of 1983 I started law school for the

second time. Even though I was working every weekend the studies went well. I formed a study group and one member of our group was the older Chinese student who had also been given a second chance. My guess is that we were both in the top half of our class and in 1986 we both graduated.

Graduation from Law School

Although our studies went well, there were significant financial obstacles to overcome. The first arose out of the purchase of the MURBS some seven years earlier.

In the early 1980's we received a letter from the tax department. I cannot remember the exact number but we were informed that approximately $8,000 in tax was owed.

The builder had declared bankruptcy before the units were built and so we never did receive title. The tax department took the position that because we never received title, we were not entitled to the tax deduction. We took the position that the down payments were a business loss and therefore should not be taxable in any event.

One day Joyce wrote a check. It was returned marked "Insufficient Funds." We called the bank. They informed us that the tax department had garnisheed the money and the account was closed. It had been the money from the sale of our home in Westridge. I don't know if the tax department acted properly, but it didn't matter. The money was gone. We had nothing. Although this was now the third time that we started with nothing, we had never before asked either of our parents for money, but now we had no choice.

We told my parents what we had lost. We told them that our only source of income was from our two part-time jobs and family allowance. We told them about our expenses that included our mortgage payments, Christian school tuition and daily expenses. They listened. They acknowledged that except for some college tuition, I had cost them very little. They admired how we had managed under difficult circumstances. They said that they had assisted three of my four brothers in the purchase of their farms and now it was our turn. That day they gave us cash for all the money we had lost.

It was a wonderful gift but where could we keep it? Any bank deposit was obviously exposed to the tax department. We did not want to keep it in the house for fear of fire or theft. In the end we put it in a bottle and buried it in the backyard. Whenever we needed some extra money, I dug up the piggy bank.

Although we had not asked Joyce's parents for money, they had over the years been very generous. Each year they gave us a significant financial gift. These gifts continued throughout law school. The monies received from our parents enabled me to finish law school. No gift was appreciated more.

The second major financial obstacle arose out of the purchase of the lakefront property. For five years we made every effort to sell the lots. While in law school I would often drive to Buck Lake to show the property. It was a three-hour round trip. The purchase of the property as well as the costs of the subdivision and the road had been financed by the Edmonton Christian Credit Union and the sale of any lot was subject to their approval. All monies would be used to pay down debt. While in law school, I was able to secure two offers but the Credit Union refused to approve either of them.

At the beginning of my final year the manager called and requested another meeting. When I arrived there was also a board member present. The meeting was an inquisition. They demanded to know where we worked, our salaries, our savings and our bank accounts. They threatened to sue. They said our credit would be ruined. I told them I would be happy to sign over all our interest in the property to them but they refused. I reminded them that I had already brought them two offers. I also informed them that I had only one year left. Thereafter, I would be able to work full-time. Nevertheless, two days before Christmas we were served with a Statement of Claim.

I made an appointment with Ben Vanden Brink. I had known him for a long time and he had assisted me in a number of real estate transactions. He reviewed our situation. He strongly recommended that we declare bankruptcy. He gave us the name of a bankruptcy trustee and the next day we met with him. The bankruptcy moved slowly and it was not until the next year that we were finally discharged.

After graduation I began my articles with the Federal Department of Justice. Articles are an apprenticeship program for lawyers, providing practical experience. At the end of one year the student must pass a series of written exams. Once passed, the student is

236

"called to the bar," joins the Law Society, and is free to practice law.

I was called to the bar on July 31, 1987. It was the same day that a tornado swept through the eastern part of Edmonton, killing 27 people and injuring 253. At that time, it was the second deadliest tornado in Canadian history.

While at the Justice Department, I received a call from Ben Vanden Brink. He was now in Red Deer. He had started his own firm and had a number of lawyers working for him. He needed a trial lawyer and asked if I would be interested in joining him. Needless to say I was more than interested. This was my goal.

After the phone call the tears of relief began to flow. I quickly closed the door so that no one would see me. It had been some thirty years earlier that I sat huddled in front of the radio and a particular program had created within me an insatiable desire to become a trial lawyer. Now I had just been offered the opportunity to end up where I had hoped to be. For the first time I allowed myself to acknowledge how much I had always wanted it.

In my mind I reviewed the thirty year detour and the factors that had brought it about. One factor was of course, my youthful hedonistic approach to life, and the price paid for in grades. I wondered whether events would have transpired differently had I been allowed to skip grade four.

I thought about what I had lost , and about what might have been. However, I found it difficult to quantify what never was, so I began to think of what I had gained. I knew that but for the detour I would never have had the family I now have. It was enough; the detour had been more than worth it. In fact, I now had the opportunity to enjoy the best of both worlds. That day I left the office early and when my family came home I was there for them.

Joyce and I were not entirely sure that we wanted to live in Red Deer; accordingly, only I moved. Joyce remained in Edmonton. I saw her and the children on weekends.

Being in Red Deer on my own turned out to be ideal because it enabled me to work sixteen hours a day. I was provided with files ordinarily conducted by senior lawyers. The learning curve was steep, but I was up for it. What made it easier was that I loved the practice of law, and unlike many lawyers I was comfortable in the courtroom. I am by nature competitive and I enjoyed the contest. The secret is to be prepared and I always was. The courtroom suited my personality perfectly.

Red Deer is a convenient city, located halfway between Edmonton and Calgary. At the time it had a population of about 75,000 people. It is large enough to have everything but small enough to make travel quick and easy. Within a month or two, I knew that I wanted to continue to practice law in Red Deer. However, by that time the children were in school in Edmonton and we didn't want to transfer them mid-year. Once the school year was over, Joyce, Laura and Chad moved to Red Deer. Delbert and Vincent were no longer at home.

Next to the ministry, moving to Red Deer marked the beginning of the happiest period in our life. Joyce did what she could to support my practice. Eventually she worked part-time in the office. Although the work may not have been as fulfilling as the ministry, she was content. For the first time in many years we had time for each other.

Although I practiced both criminal and civil law, I found criminal law the most interesting. Also the stakes were higher. Generally speaking, in civil law the issue is; "how much money" does the client get? In criminal law the issue is; "how much time?"

Before I describe the nature of my practice, I want to say something about two of the lawyers I was practicing with: Ben Vanden Brink and Brad Willis.

Two Lawyers

Ben Vanden Brink is without doubt one of the most

exceptional people I have met. Most lawyers begin their careers by working as associates in various law firms. If the firm values their work, they are often invited to become partners. Ben began his career as a partner with a large firm in Edmonton. He is brilliant, with a personality to match. In a crowd he moves easily, always with grace and style. He has a wonderful sense of humor. Because of his larger-than-life personality, he was an exceptional rainmaker.

He was also the best negotiator I have ever met. As a negotiator he was resourceful and creative. To his employees he was fair, considerate and generous. He is helpful and positive. As far as he was concerned, mistakes were to be corrected, not criticized. As a business partner, he was honest, loyal and reliable. He always kept his word. I learned from him that, as between partners, negotiations should always be on a win-win basis. As long as I have known him, we have never had a harsh word. I could not have been more fortunate than to begin my career with him.

Brad Willis knew the law better than any other lawyer I know. He constantly read law books, many of which dealt with the history of law. He would often quote old English judges at length. He was a speed-reader and in a short time he could consume an enormous amount of information. He quickly understood the issues. In court, he was responsive to any question a judge might ask. His answers were concise and to the point.

He intimidated the other lawyers. When they presented their case, he often objected, either on points of law or fact. In supporting his objections, he would reference obscure cases. He seemed always to have his opposition reeling.

Unfortunately, he also had a flaw. Although he loved trials, he hated taking those steps necessary to bring a matter to trial. As a result his files floundered and his clients were unhappy.

Years later I learned that he had been disbarred. Apparently, he had been so tardy that a number of his clients had reported him to the Law Society. In some cases limitation dates had been ignored, causing his clients to lose by default.

Notwithstanding his flaws, he and I worked well together. I was relentless in moving files forward. If I thought the opposing lawyer was stalling, I would immediately apply to the court for deadlines. Most of my cases were resolved in less than half the time it took others.

Within a few years Ben, Brad and I formed a partnership. Unfortunately the partnership did not go well. Almost all the issues arose out of Brad's failure to advance his files. The partnership lasted only a few months. After one confrontational meeting, Brad left.

Civil Litigation

Prior to his departure, Brad and I had already completed two trials. Both were my cases and I had asked Brad to assist me. The first trial involved a farmer who had lost in excess of $750,000. One defendant was a mortgage company. I believe that the facts were that the mortgage company had invested $250,000 of his funds in mortgages that turned out to be worthless. The remaining $500,000 was deposited in a bank. The mortgage company then declared bankruptcy, and the bank seized the $500,000 to satisfy a loan made by them to the mortgage company. The issue was whether, in respect to the $250,000, the mortgage company had done its due diligence. If not, had it breached its duty to the farmer?

The second defendant was the bank for both the farmer and the mortgage company. The issues were whether in respect to the $250,000, the bank knew that the money invested by the mortgage company belonged to the farmer; and did the bank know the risky nature of the investments? If so, did the bank breach its duty to the farmer in failing to warn him? In respect to the $500,000, did the bank know that the money was initially given to the mortgage company? If so, it was trust money, in which case it would belong to the farmer. The judge found against both defendants. The farmer received his money.

In the second trial my brother Melvin was the plaintiff. He owned a farm on which he raised a large number of hogs. On one occasion he purchased hogs from an auction mart. They were suffering from a type of pneumonia that was a "reportable" disease. The disease was such that the hogs could appear to be healthy. (Legislation required that if any person knew of animals that had a "reportable" disease, they were required to report it.) As a result, his existing herd became infected. Because it was a "reportable" disease, the Department of Agriculture destroyed his entire herd. He received no compensation.

The defendants were the previous owners of the hogs, the auction mart, and an employee of the auction mart. It was the employee's job to encourage farmers to sell their hogs through the auction mart. The issue was whether any or all the defendants knew that the hogs purchased by Melvin had the disease. If so, were they responsible for Melvin's loss? The judge found that all the defendants knew, and all had a duty to report. The breach of that duty made them all responsible for Melvin's loss.

* * * * *

After Brad left, Ben and I formed a new partnership. Although Ben was probably a better rainmaker, the fact was, we were both good.

PORCOFF

In one case a group of unhappy farmers came to see me. I cannot remember the exact details, but I believe their story went something like this.

Peter Pocklington owned Gainers, a slaughtering plant in Edmonton. The relationship between management and labor was acidic. There were strikes and lockouts; Pocklington threatened to close the plant. Gainers was the only large processing plant for hogs in Alberta but it was no longer reliable. If Gainers closed, farmers would be required to ship their hogs out of province. The cost of transportation would go up and in transit the hogs would lose weight so the farmers would receive less for each hog.

The farmers complained to the provincial government. It was agreed that another slaughtering plant was necessary. The government would support the purchase and expansion of an existing facility in Red Deer called "Fletchers". To ensure a steady supply of hogs, the farmers were promised a certain number of shares based on the number of hogs shipped to Fletchers. I do not remember the ratio. The plant was purchased and expanded, and the farmers responded. For reasons no longer in memory, the shares were not issued. It may have been that Gainers had already closed and so Fletchers would get the hogs in any event.

The farmers wanted to hire me. The purpose was to compel Fletchers or the government to issue the shares. The problem was, how could such an effort be financed? At the time the value of the shares was unknown because none had been issued. The cost of a large-scale lawsuit could not possibly be borne by a few farmers. What made matters worse was that some of the members on the Fletchers' board of directors were farmers from the various regions of the province.

Eventually we reached an agreement. The farmers who came to see me would organize meetings throughout the province. They would concentrate on those regions where the majority of the hogs were grown. I would speak and answer questions. The organizers would then ask others to join the group. The name of our group was "PORCOFF," (Producer's Organization to Regain Control of Fletchers). The cost of joining was $500.

There were many meetings and I have long ago forgotten most of them, but there are two that I remember. The first meeting was somewhere east of Edmonton and within the region of one of the Fletchers' board of directors. I believe his name was something like Ukimchuk, but I am no longer sure. One of our group warned me that

Ukimchuk would likely try to undermine our attempt to recruit supporters. He said that Ukimchuk was one of the most aggressive people he had ever met.

Another member of our group (who was a past member of the Fletchers' board of directors) had previously given me all the minutes of the board. He also gave me a letter that he had received from Ukimchuk while they were on the board together. From the minutes I could identify all the board members who supported our position and those who opposed it. Ukimchuk was clearly opposed. I highlighted all the statements and votes that could be attributed to him.

I had not met Ukimchuk before, so prior to the meeting someone pointed him out. He was a short, overweight, angry looking person. During my speech he regularly interrupted me. He was loud and bombastic. He challenged everything I said. On several occasions he was asked to reserve his comments until after I was finished, but he refused.

Then it became personal. He said that in his opinion I didn't give a damn about the farmers. The only person to benefit from joining our group was me. He said that he believed that the farmers should be given the shares, but that hiring an opportunistic, gold-digging lawyer was not the answer. As a board member he had worked tirelessly on behalf of the farmers and if they wanted the shares they should support him and not some over-rated lawyer.

I heard enough. I took the minutes from my brief-case and began quoting from them. I cited the number of times that he had voted against issuing the shares to the farmers.

While I was reading from the minutes, Ukimchuk tried to stop me. He likely knew what was coming. "Where did you get the minutes?" he shouted repeatedly. "They're private. Why should we hear this bullshit if you won't tell us how you got them. Did you steal them?"

Then I read from the letter. In the letter he was trying to persuade the other board member to also vote against issuing the shares. He pointed out that from Fletchers' point of view issuing the shares would be a logistical nightmare. Detailed records would have to be kept of all contributors, which would include their names, addresses and phone numbers. Fletchers would also have to keep a record of all the hogs contributed by each farmer. This number would change on almost a weekly basis. He then concluded his letter by saying; "besides, most of the farmers are too damn stupid to know what a share looks like. They will probably use it for ass-wipe."

When I finished reading everyone was quiet, even Ukimchuk. Then someone stood up, pointed at him and said, "you two-faced son-of-a-bitch, I think you should leave." Ukimchuk's only response was to say, "I want to see the letter first," but it was too late. Almost everyone was now shouting at him. Some were cursing but most were demanding that he leave. He eventually did. A few followed him. I could hear the sound of argument coming from the hallway.

Several months later I was told that Ukimchuk had sold his farm and moved to Edmonton. The person who told me wasn't sure if it had anything to do with the meeting, but he thought it did.

On another occasion Fletchers held a general meeting in Lethbridge and all hog producers were invited to attend. A member of our group had informed Ben and me of the meeting and we decided to attend. Because of the share issue the meeting was well attended. Fletchers wanted to talk about the wonderful service they were providing but the farmers wanted to talk about the shares.

Prior to the meeting one of our group had requested that we be permitted to speak. His request was denied but he was not deterred. After the meeting began, he announced that Ben and I were present. He again asked permission for us to speak. Again permission was flatly denied. We had anticipated their response so the previous day we had arranged to rent a large community hall directly across the street. When permission was denied, the same individual announced that we would be speaking at the community hall across the street in about ten minutes. Almost everyone left and crossed the street. I spoke. Both Ben and I answered questions. Many farmers joined. It was the single most successful fund-raising event.

There are a number of Hutterite colonies in southern Alberta. These are religious groups and their religious principles prohibit them from participating in a lawsuit. Consequently, they did not sign up but they did become some of the best financial contributors. All of the moneys combined, but particularly from the Lethbridge meeting, made the claim for the shares viable. Eventually, all the farmers received their shares.

The Regina Meeting

The 1980's were a terrible time for farmers. In 1981 the interest rate exceeded 20%. The economy was in recession and many farmers had been foreclosed on. A few had even committed suicide. One of the worst hit areas was Saskatchewan.

Some farmers came to see us for legal help because we were often able to negotiate agreements with the banks. Typically the farmers would retain their home quarter and in exchange they promised not to fight the foreclosure on any other land they owned. The

Saskatchewan government assisted by introducing new programs, which in effect, mandated meaningful negotiations prior to foreclosure.

Each year, one of the largest agricultural fairs in Canada is held in Regina. In about 1990 the government sponsored various meetings to be held during the fair to explain the benefits of their new program. The banks had also been invited to speak. Ben and I attended. In the morning the government advertised their new programs and the bankers talked about their efforts to make things better. No one had been scheduled to speak for the farmers.

A group of farmers told the organizers that we were present. They pointed out that no one had been scheduled to speak for them and they asked that we be permitted to do so. This time permission was granted. It was announced that we would speak at 1:30 p.m. and the word was out. Soon flyers appeared announcing that two lawyers from Red Deer would speak. The meeting was packed – there may have been as many as 500 people. This time Ben spoke.

He said that if someone had been able to fly over Europe in the middle ages, they would have noted that all the largest buildings were churches and cathedrals. Why was that so? It was because the churches owned much of the land. They were profiting from the farmers who paid the rent. If one were to fly over Canada today, they would note that some of the largest buildings were banks. Why was that so? The reasons were the same. They were profiting from the farmers. The speech was pure theater but the farmers loved it. Ben received a long, enthusiastic standing ovation. The bankers remained seated.

After the meeting, it seemed as if all the farmers wanted us to represent them but there was a problem. Although the work was rewarding, it was not profitable. Farmers facing foreclosure have no money. Of the many who wanted us to represent them, we selected only five.

A Criminal Trial

I conducted many criminal trials. People often ask how I could defend guilty people? My answer is:

1. It is not for me to decide guilt;

2. Every person, even the guilty person, is entitled to the presumption of innocence until proven guilty; and

3. Every person, including a defense lawyer, is obligated to operate under that assumption until the person is found guilty.

Six of the trials were jury trials and none were lost. What follows is a summary of one of the trials.

Late one afternoon I met with Henry and Edith Beckworth. Both were in their early sixties. Before moving to Red Deer, they had lived in a small town in the Alberta foothills. They had raised four daughters. He had worked for a cement manufacturing company, operating a front-end loader.

Her job ceased to exist when she was about 55. Given her age, she was unable to find other work. They decided that until Henry retired, she would care for two children from a neighboring family. The girl whom we will call Mary was about five years old and her brother was about two. The parents dropped the children off at about 7:30 a.m. The children loved the Beckworths. They called them grandpa and grandma. The Beckworths also loved the children.

Henry worked days and was generally home by 5:00 p.m. Whenever he worked overtime, he would first return home for dinner and then go back to work. One day an emergency arose and he was required to work until 1:00 a.m. so the next day he slept in.

When the children arrived, they were told to be quiet because grandpa was sleeping. Occasionally they would peek through the bedroom door to see if he was up. At about 11:00 a.m. he did get up. He was sitting in a wicker chair at the foot of the bed. "Grandpa is up," they shouted when they saw him. They opened the bedroom door and rushed in to hug him.

He was still wearing his pajamas. It was worn thin and ripped in all the wrong places. As such, it revealed more than it concealed. He quickly ushered the children out of the bedroom, but in doing so he may have revealed even more. He closed the door and changed into his work clothes.

Later that summer Henry retired as planned. They moved to Red Deer because two of their daughters already lived there. In the meantime Mary began kindergarten. One day her teacher chose to teach from a program called a "Care Kit." It was an attempt to teach children the difference between good and bad touching. It consisted of a number of posters showing adults touching children. These posters were shown to the children. On the back of the posters was some pre-printed material that the teacher read. After each poster was shown and the material read, the children would be asked whether what they saw was good or bad touching.

At the end of the class the teacher asked whether any of them had ever been touched in a bad way. All the children said no. She then asked if any of them had ever touched someone else in a bad way and Mary put up her hand. The teacher ushered her to the principal's office. The principal took a statement. The girl told the principal that she had touched Henry's private part when she

253

hugged him. After taking the statement, the principal called both parents and social services. Everyone rushed to the school. A social worker took another statement and this time Mary said that she touched Henry twice and that Henry had asked her to.

The social worker called the police. A police officer hurried to the school. She took another statement. This time Mary said that she had touched Henry more than twice. She didn't know the number but he had asked her to do it and that wasn't all. She then went on to describe various other "bad touchings."

Because the Beckworths were now living in Red Deer, the Red Deer police were called. They were asked to obtain a statement from Henry if possible. They called Henry and asked if he would meet with them at the police station. They did not say why. Edith went with him but she was not permitted in the interview room. Apparently he was read his rights, but Henry does not remember. At this point it is necessary to know two things about Henry.

He is a severe diabetic. He and Edith always ate dinner at 5:30 p.m. Failure to eat on time would gradually lead to a diabetic stupor. As 5:30 approached, Edith began to worry. She went to the front desk and told another officer about Henry's condition. She was assured it would not be long. She asked why they wanted to see Henry, but they refused to tell her. Time passed and by

6:00 p.m. she was frantic. She knew that Henry would not be well. Again she expressed her concerns. The answers were the same. Finally at 6:30 p.m. they brought Henry to the front. He was supported by a police officer. Henry could hardly talk; he slurred every word. They raced home.

Henry also has a significant mental impairment. Approximately ten years after they were married, he had been hit on the side of the head with a swing boom. He had been hospitalized for weeks; thereafter, Edith cared for him. We had him tested prior to trial and his I.Q. was 80. Because of his impairment Edith made all the decisions.

Physically he recovered. Before the accident Henry had operated a front-end loader and after his recovery he applied for his old job back. The company tested him, and found his skills to be barely adequate. Nonetheless they hired him. Over time he learned to operate the machine well.

The day after his visit to the police station, Henry was arrested and charged with sexual assault. We learned later that the police officer had taken a thirty-six-page statement from him. Most of the statement consisted of a transcript from a tape recording.

At the beginning of the interview Henry steadfastly denied having ever touched Mary in an inappropriate manner. However, as the interview continued the police officer became more aggressive. At the same time Henry's capacity to resist diminished. The police officer knew that the Beckworths loved Mary and he repeatedly tried to use that against Henry. What follows is a synopsis of the interview.

"Do you love Mary?"

"Yes."

"Has she ever lied to you?"

"No."

"As far as you know has she ever lied to someone else?"

"No."

"So if she were to say something about you it would be true, is that right?"

"Yes."

"She said she touched your private parts, is that right?"

"If she said she did than she probably did."

"So you admit it?"

"Yes, if she said she did."

"She also said that you asked her to touch you, is that right?"

"No."

"So you're saying she is a liar, is that right?"

"No."

"You say she isn't a liar, but you also say that what she said is not true. Which is it?"

"Mary is not a liar."

"Did you ever touch her?"

"No."

"You mean that all the time she was at your place you never touched her?"

"Yes I did touch her but...." The police officer interrupted him.

"So she is telling the truth."

"Yes. If she says that I touched her than I probably did. She is not a liar."

And so it went until the police officer had Henry admitting to everything that Mary said happened. Henry then signed the statement which was in effect a confession.

After the police had obtained what they wanted, the officer insisted that Henry apologize to the girl's parents. The officer called the parents and put Henry on the line. He apologized.

During my interview with Henry and Edith, he insisted that he had never asked Mary to touch him. Neither had he ever touched her in an inappropriate manner. He told me about his pajamas. He said it was possible that she had touched him. He also said that he remembered the first half of the police interview but not the last half.

I sensed that he was telling the truth so I agreed to act for him. It turned out to be the highlight of my career. I phoned the prosecuting attorney. He sent me all the statements Mary had given as well as Henry's statement.

In almost all criminal cases there is a preliminary hearing for a judge to assess whether there is sufficient evidence for a trial. It was during that hearing that we learned about the Care Kit. After the hearing we obtained the entire Care Kit from the Department of Education.

In every trial the prosecutor presents his or her case first. After each witness the defense is permitted to cross-examine. Mary's testimony was similar to the statement she had given the police officer. During cross-examination she said she had not told the teacher, principal or the social worker everything because she was afraid. She denied describing what she had seen on the posters, but did admit that she was "thinking about them" when she talked to the police officer. From our point of view the other important witness was the female police officer who took the first statement. During cross-examination she acknowledged that when she took the statement it had not occurred to her that Mary might have been describing the various touchings that she had just seen on the posters of the Care Kit.

After the prosecutor finished presenting his case it was our turn. We began by calling the psychiatrist who had previously tested Henry. A psychiatrist is both a medical doctor and a psychologist. As such, he could testify on the effects of diabetes as well as Henry's mental capacities.

One question that every defense lawyer must decide is whether to put the accused on the stand. I decided Henry would testify. I believed he was honest. I wanted the jury to hear him.

The prosecutor had been aggressive throughout the trial. I knew that Henry sometimes had trouble understanding a question, which could hurt him. His claim that he had no memory of part of the police interview might also hurt him. It was a chance we had to take. However, after the very first question from the prosecutor, I knew that Henry would be all right. The question was: "We have heard evidence that you don't know much. Is that true?" he snarled.

"People say that I don't know. But I don't know that I don't know," was the soft reply.

Of all the answers I had heard in all the trials I had conducted, this answer was the most profound. And that was from a man with an I.Q. of 80.

After we had presented our defense, the jury was excused for the night. The next day both sides would have the opportunity to address the jury. I spoke for eight hours. We broke only for lunch. I went through each statement, line by line. I reviewed all the evidence favorable to Henry.

Once all the evidence was in, two things became

clear:

1. Mary's statement was a fabrication. When she gave her statement to the principal, she said that she had touched Henry's private part. That may have been true. Everything added thereafter was false. She was telling everyone what she thought they wanted to hear. In fact her statement to the police correlated almost perfectly to the posters she had just seen.

2. Henry's statement was unreliable. It was mainly a transcript from a tape. Unfortunately, once the statement was completed, the tape had been destroyed. But even without the tape, it was obvious that Henry was descending into a diabetic stupor. He was becoming less responsive. The longer the interview, the more he slurred his words. Near the end he was almost unintelligible.

I spent the evening with Henry and his extended family. I told them to prepare for the worst. Henry and Edith had several grandchildren. All were young. It was agreed that the sons-in-laws would leave with the grandchildren. The daughters wanted to stay. Each time another grandchild said good-bye there was another flood of tears. The hugs and kisses seemed to continue forever. After the grandchildren left, the tears flowed even more freely, especially from the daughters. Henry and Edith had raised their children as Christians. They belonged to a group that did not believe in organized Christianity. Each Sunday they would go to the home of a like-minded couple and they would worship together.

Every once in a while one or another of the daughters would drop to her knees and pray. When I left the daughters were still there.

The next morning the prosecutor spoke for about an hour. Basically his message was that Henry's diabetes and mental capacity were no excuse for his bad behavior. When he was done, the judge addressed the jury. Everything was done by noon. It was now in the hands of the jury. The trial had lasted two weeks.

Throughout much of the trial my daughter Laura was present. While the jury was deliberating we went to a movie. Late that afternoon we received a message. The jury had reached a verdict. We quickly reconvened. Edith and the daughters were present but none of the grandchildren. The jury announced their verdict. Not guilty.

I had previously asked everyone to retain their composure, whatever the verdict. They tried, but their joy could not be contained. They shouted, they cried, they laughed, they hugged and they celebrated. Henry wept. Edith prayed. She had not forgotten whom to thank. After a short time, we stepped into the hallway. Unknown to us, nine of the twelve jurors had waited for Henry and his family. Some hugged him. Some said they hoped he could get on with his life. All wished him well.

In part, I treasure this case because Laura was present much of the time. Unlike many occupations (such as farming, carpentry, electrical or plumbing), the children of professional people rarely see their parents work. As such they cannot always appreciate the skill with which their parents operate. In this case, however, my daughter was there. She had witnessed my finest hour.

* * * * * *

One of the reasons I enjoyed practicing with Ben, was that both of us have retained a bit of a mischievous and adventurous nature. In February 1988, the Winter Olympics were held in Calgary, Alberta. Many people volunteered as language interpreters. Most were needed at the Calgary airport to be available to the athletes, coaches and dignitaries who arrived by plane.

I cannot remember why, but during that time Ben and I happened to be at the airport. It was approximately 9:00 p.m. There was one sign near one of the information desks that caught our attention. It said that there were interpreters available for all the major languages in the world. We decided to test it.

Ben was born in the Netherlands and arrived in Canada as a teenager. He knew the Dutch language well. I was born in Canada, but my grandparents spoke Dutch in their home. As such, I learned to understand the Dutch language, but speaking it was more difficult. We decided to pretend to be two Dutch speed-skating coaches. We walked to the information desk and, in broken English, asked for a Dutch interpreter.

The lady behind the desk was surprised. Although she could not speak Dutch, she knew what we wanted. She was sorry but there were no Dutch interpreters available. She checked the incoming flights, but there were none scheduled to arrive from the Netherlands. That was why there was no one available.

She ushered us to an exclusive lounge. There was no one there. She told us to make ourselves comfortable and she would get us an interpreter. In the meantime we could order whatever food or drink we wished. She gave us a menu for both. There would be no charge. Ben thought he had taken a short cut to paradise. He had all the free, good quality scotch he wanted. Even I had a drink, although it probably wasn't scotch.

We talked about what we would say when the interpreter arrived. There were no attractive options, so we decided to leave early, but we did leave a note written in Dutch. We told them that we had made our own arrangements, and we couldn't wait. We then left $40 for their trouble, and wished them a good day. Ben signed using only his first name.

* * * * *

In 1988-89, Vincent was attending Calvin College in Grand Rapids, Michigan. Joyce and I decided to visit him. The itinerary was such that the last portion of the flight was from Toronto to Grand Rapids, with a stop in Saginaw, Michigan.

The plane was a small 16-passenger plane. There were approximately 12 passengers on board. Joyce was the only woman. There were no flight attendants. The first sign of trouble was on the final approach in Saginaw. The pilot aborted the landing and pulled up. He announced that his instruments indicated that the landing gear was not in the locked position. He then began to fly in circles around the control tower, in such a way as to expose the belly of the plane to the tower. We could see the traffic controller look at our plane with binoculars.

After several passes the pilot informed us that the front landing gear was only partially down. He would continue to try to fix the problem. He also told us that it would be necessary to burn off some fuel before attempting a landing. Thereafter, we flew in wide circles around Saginaw. Occasionally the pilot flew past the control tower, each time exposing the belly of the plane to the controller. This continued for about 45 minutes. In the meantime we noticed a number of vehicles parking alongside the runway. Eventually there were fire trucks, police cars, ambulances and rescue vehicles.

The pilot informed us that he had been unable to fix the problem and that we were to prepare for an emergency landing. He told us to fasten our seatbelts as tightly as possible and lean forward with our head between our knees. He also told us where the exit doors were. Everyone did as they were told. Apart from the pilot's voice, no one made a sound. When the pilot announced that we were on final approach, Joyce and I held hands but said nothing. It wasn't necessary.

The approach was a period of anxious uncertainty. The landing was rough. The front of the plane dropped but did not strike the runway. The partially lowered landing gear was apparently holding up but the wheel was obviously not parallel to the plane. As soon as it made contact with the runway, the plane lurched to the side, nearly striking a fire truck. The pilot corrected and we were now traveling in a zigzag pattern down the runway.

Eventually we came to rest near the terminal. No one had made a sound. The pilot walked to the rear of the cabin to open the door. He was drenched in sweat. Perhaps he, more than anyone else, had realized the gravity of the situation.

After we deplaned, all the passengers walked quietly to the bar, with the exception of Joyce and I. We sat in the terminal to consider our options. Shortly thereafter a company representative approached us. He asked if we were on the flight that had just landed. We said yes. He asked where we were going. We told him Grand Rapids. That day, there were no subsequent flights to Grand Rapids so we went by taxi, paid for by the company.

In the meantime Vince was at the airport to pick us up. There were no cell phones so we were unable to communicate with him. We told the cab driver to take us directly to his dorm, which he did. We went to his room and met his roommate. Shorty after we arrived, Vince phoned his roommate to ask if he had heard from us.

Recently, Joyce and I discussed what we thought about while we were flying around Saginaw. The following are her thoughts in her own words. "Most of the time I was praying for a safe landing. I wasn't afraid of dying, but I still had so much to live for. None of the children were married and I wanted to be at their weddings. I wanted to see them get established in their careers and be an influence in the lives of their children."

My thoughts were less noble. I did not expect that

we would crash, but I thought about the various possibilities if we did. I would either survive or die. If I died, so be it. But if I survived, what could I do? I made sure that I knew where the doors were. I thought about how I could help Joyce, especially if there was a rush for the doors. My biggest concern was fire. I looked for the fire extinguishers. I could see two of them, one in the front and one in the back. I was also quite sure that there was one in the cabin, behind the pilot.

Sometime later, someone asked me if I thought about the after-life while we were flying around Saginaw. The answer was no. I knew that a crash, and therefore death, was a theoretical possibility but I never accepted it as probable or inevitable. Consequently, it never became an emotional reality.

* * * * *

In the summer of 1995, I organized a white-water rafting trip with our boys. At that time Del was practicing law in Vancouver, Vince had just completed his medical practicum, and Chad was about to enroll at Trinity Western University. We were to raft down the Kicking Horse River near the town of Golden B.C.. Del drove from Vancouver, and Vince, Chad and I drove from Edmonton. We met in Golden the evening before the event.

The first morning was uneventful. We met the

group we were to raft with. There were about fifty of us and we were transported by bus to the launching area. There we were introduced to the guides and given some safety instructions. We were then divided up into five smaller groups of about ten rafters. We were given helmets, wet suits and life jackets. Each group was assigned a guide and a raft. About mid-morning we pushed off.

As we were rafting, we learned more about our guide. He was a university student from Calgary. We all liked him. He was adventurous and personable. He told us that his father had come to watch him guide and was videotaping us as we rafted down the river. From time to time we would see his father on the shore with his camera.

At noon we stopped for lunch. We were told that we were approaching the most challenging part of the river. It included an area known as the "devil's drop." They assured us that although the drop was challenging none of their rafts had ever overturned. Shortly after lunch we again pushed off. There were two rafts ahead of us and two behind. As we were rafting our guide told us that his father was standing on the shore just above the devil's drop and would be videotaping our passage through the drop.

Two members of our group were a couple. Both were somewhat overweight, although he more so than her. He was short and weighed well over 200 pounds. I have long ago forgotten their names so I will call them Jake and Judy. As we approached the drop we could see the previous rafts disappear from view. We were next. Jake and Judy were clearly apprehensive.

The drop was not long, perhaps only six feet; nonetheless, the water was extremely turbulent. The waters were moving in all directions and the raft was responding. When we hit the bottom, the raft began to twist sideways. Without warning a wall of water gripped the side of the raft and turned it upside down.

I continued to hold on to the ropes that ran along the length of the raft. The raft propelled out of the drop and floated on the swiftly running river. Once we were out of the drop, the water was turbulent but not deep. As a result, I was being dragged over the rocks. Eventually I was able to surface and saw Vincent. He was standing on the upside-down raft, holding on to Jake. Ordinarily, it would have been impossible to pull such a heavy weight out of a raging river onto a slippery, bouncing raft. But as I watched, Vincent did just that. He reached down and grabbed the strap of Jake's life jacket and heaved him onto the raft. He then assisted me onto the raft, and then the guide.

By this time there were four of us on the raft, but Del and Chad were still missing, as was Judy. Jake kept telling us that she could not swim. Then at the side of the raft Judy and Del popped up. They had been under the raft the whole time; their heads in the cavity where our feet had previously been.

It was only later that we learned what happened. When the raft overturned, Judy had grabbed onto Del. Both then surfaced under the raft, but they were also being dragged over the rocks. Judy was fighting hard to hold onto Del so he tried to settle her down.

"Can you hear me?" he called out in the darkness.

"Yes," she answered back, "but I can't swim."

"I'm a life guard," he shouted. "You will be okay, if you do as I say. On the count of three, take a deep breath. Hold on to me, but don't fight, and I'll pull you to the other side."

"Okay," she responded fearfully.

Del took hold of her life jacket, and on the count of three pulled her under the water. Even though he had told her not to fight, she did anyway. She tried to wrap her arms around him, nearly immobilizing his free arm. Nonetheless he was able to seize the rope and together they came up. Vincent was the first to see her, and he pulled her onto the raft. I assisted Del. When Judy saw Jake she cried.

There were now six of us on the overturned raft, but Chad was not one of them. We could see a few heads bobbing in the water but with their helmets on it was impossible to recognize anyone. One person was hanging on to an overhanging branch near the shore; the following raft picked two up. But that accounted for only nine, and we had started with ten. Then we saw Chad swimming toward us. The guide helped him onto the raft.

When the lead guide in the first raft saw us overturn he immediately beached his raft on a sandbar in the middle of the river. As we drifted by, he threw a rope to us and our guide fastened it to our raft. In the meantime, the lead guide was attempting to fasten his end of the rope to a log that was lying on the sandbar. As he was winding the rope around the log, the rope jerked tight. His finger was caught between the log and the rope, and instantly broke.

All of the rafts congregated on the sandbar. Our guide quickly did a head count and everyone was accounted for. As it turned out, other than the lead guide, no one was hurt. The wet suits and life jackets had protected us from the rocks. That evening the boys and I had dinner together. It was more somber than the previous dinner, but it was interesting to hear each person's account of what had happened. I was so very thankful that all the boys are excellent swimmers. The summers they had spent in our Westridge pool had paid off.

271

Whitewater rafting on the Kicking Horse River

The next and final day we were back on the river. There were, however, two people missing from our group. Jake and Judy did not return. The rafting itself was uneventful and relaxing. We were done rafting by 4:00 p.m. The boys and I had an early dinner, after which we said our goodbyes. Unfortunately the devil of misfortune had one more visit to make.

We returned home at about midnight. Joyce was still up and told us that Karen (Del's wife) had called. Del had been involved in a car accident, and he was returning home by bus. We called Karen back but she had little additional information. She did say that Del was okay.

The next morning Del called and told us what happened. Because he and Karen had only one car, he had borrowed his father-in-law's car to get to Golden. It was a 1986 Nissan 300ZX twin turbo. Del was told that the tires were in poor shape. Nonetheless, he took the car. He referred to the trip to Golden as the best drive in his life. It was hot and he had taken the t-roof off.

On the last afternoon of our rafting trip it had rained. Del could tell that the car was hydroplaning wherever water had collected on the asphalt. He had thought about turning back but he knew that we had already left in the opposite direction, so he decided to continue. Approximately 30 minutes out of Golden he was driving down a long hill. At the base of the hill was a bridge, after which the highway turned right. He was doing about 60 km per hour over the bridge. Thereafter he accelerated but he did not quickly enough see a pool of water on the road. The car hydroplaned and began to spin on the highway.

On the left hand side of the highway was a rock wall. On the right was a ditch. Fortunately the car spun into the ditch and then launched onto a level lot that was used to store sand for winter roads. By the time the car came to rest, three of the tires had been ripped off the rims and there was significant damage to the undercarriage.

Had the accident occurred two minutes later Del would have been driving along Beaver Canyon, which is one of the deepest canyons on the Trans-Canada Highway. In some places the canyon is hundreds of feet deep. Every time I drive by that spot, my stomach turns a bit when I think about what might have been.

* * * * *

Although I very much enjoyed my practice with Ben, I began to realize that I could not continue as before. Neither bankrupt farmers nor criminals have any money. I would never be able to retire if we continued as we were.

Conducting a practice in many areas of law is very difficult. Law was changing quickly and keeping up with the changes was time consuming. Consequently, I wanted to specialize in litigation and personal injury, to the exclusion of all else. Ben disagreed. He believed that we should keep all options open. Neither could convince the other. With regret we separated.

Thereafter events transpired quickly. I moved into my own office and Joyce became my bookkeeper. Although I continued to do civil litigation, the majority of my practice arose out of personal injury cases. I also began to advertise on a local television station, which was very effective.

One day a husband and wife walked into my office. They had recently emigrated from Sudan. He was a very large man, well over six feet tall and nearly 300 pounds. Next to him she seemed tiny but on her own she was about average. She was strikingly beautiful.

Generally speaking, when injured clients came in, I would begin by having them fill in a questionnaire as to the cause of the accident and the extent of the injury. They would also be required to sign a number of authorizations which would permit me to obtain the police reports and their medical records.

When I asked for various pieces of information he did all the talking, even if the question was directed at her. At first I thought that she was unable to speak English, but when they filled in the questionnaire he told her what to write in English, including information in respect to her past medical history. She would speak to him but not to me. I asked that she answer my questions directly but she simply looked at him and he refused. I told them that I could not act for her if he refused to allow her to speak to me. Eventually he agreed. However, even then when I asked her a direct question she would always look at him first. If he nodded in the affirmative she would answer, but otherwise not. I finally told them that I wanted to see them individually and if they refused they would have to find another lawyer.

He agreed so she left and I took his information

first. He was not cooperative. At first he refused to sign the authorizations. He volunteered to get the medical information and bring it to me. He said that he was unable to work as a result of the accident but refused to provide details. He offered to provide all the information in due course. I began to doubt whether he was even injured.

When it was time to get her information he refused to leave. He said that he was entitled to be there with his wife. I told him that I did not want her information influenced by him in any way. He reluctantly agreed but only if I kept the door open.

She was clearly unaccustomed to speaking for herself. At first she was hesitant and ambivalent, but eventually became more forthcoming. I believed her. She was clearly a well-educated, perceptive and intelligent woman. She spoke and wrote fluent English. She was pleasant, polite and considerate. At the time of the accident she was working as a cleaner in the hospital. She had been unable to work for a few days after the accident, but by the time she came to see me she was already back to work. She had a degree in education and hoped some day to teach. The longer I spoke with her, the more I found her to be a woman of grace and goodwill. I told her that if she ever needed a letter of recommendation I would be happy to provide one.

Eventually we settled her claim with the insurance

company. After she signed a number of documents I gave her a check and wished her well. Her husband was waiting for her in the waiting room and before they left he took the check from her.

After a while I came to realize that I could not continue to act for him. I was convinced that he had not been injured and that he was fabricating a claim. Consequently, I called him in and told him that I could no longer act for him. He asked why, so I told him. He was furious. He said that he wanted my file and would not leave without it. I told him that I would photocopy all the documents on the file, but that he could not have the original. He came around the desk and attempted to seize it. I asked my secretary to phone the police which she did. She told me that the police were on their way at which time he left.

My office was on the third floor of an office building and the elevators were slow. By the time he reached the first floor two police officers were already there and apprehended him. One officer kept him there while the other came to see me. He asked if I wanted to press charges. I said no.

Approximately a month later I learned that he was in jail awaiting trial for murder. He had shot his wife through the head.

* * * * *

In 2000, Dave MacDonell, my son-in-law, joined me. We continued to practice together until 2004. Before joining me, Dave and Laura lived in Edmonton. After Dave graduated from law school in 1999, he began his articles with a large firm but completed them with me.

Not often in life does one meet a person whose personality is marked by his willingness to please. Dave is such a person. I have never seen him deny a request for assistance. He is truly a likeable person. He is also one of the most social people I have ever met and as such, was an excellent rainmaker. He was genuinely concerned about his clients' wellbeing and worked hard on their behalf. His clients loved him. Not only was Dave a good rainmaker, his client maintenance was exceptional. He was responsive, dependable and honest.

Working with Dave was enjoyable. There is perhaps nothing that unites people more than working together to achieve a common goal. Almost every day we had lunch together. Over time we developed a warm friendship that continues to this day.

CHAPTER 9
OTHER CASES

As I thought about the various cases or files that arose during the latter part of my career, four consistently rose to the top. They had nothing to do with personal injury or civil litigation.

AN ECCLESIASTICAL CASE

Although all of the documents and matters referenced below are public, I have decided not to use the names of the parties involved. The reason is that some of the parties have sincerely apologized for their involvement in this matter.

279

Joyce and I had been members of the New Life Fellowship Christian Reformed Church (New Life) in Red Deer since 1988. From 1988 to 1997, New Life had enjoyed the leadership of a young, energetic and charismatic pastor. The worship services were upbeat, with a music ministry to match. All the services were well attended, especially by younger families. The church had grown and in 1996 a building was purchased which was then converted into a new church.

In 1997 the parishioners discovered that their pastor (hereinafter referred to as the former pastor) had been involved in an inappropriate relationship with two female members of the church. As a result he was deposed.

In the summer of 1998, a new pastor accepted the call to New Life. The new pastor also had an outgoing personality. His preaching however, was more traditional. He did not appeal to the younger people in the same way the former pastor had. He was less diplomatic and occasionally angered people whom he counseled or with whom he worked. Nonetheless, membership also grew under his leadership.

In April 2000, the new pastor called me. He was devastated. He told me that the Council of New Life was attempting to depose him. He asked for my assistance.

As a trial lawyer, I had learned that the answers to many issues can be found in the facts. Consequently, I requested all the minutes of New Life. The request was denied.

New Life had been incorporated under the Alberta Societies Act. The Act provided that any member of the church had an absolute right to the minutes. I prepared a court application to compel the church to provide the minutes. Before filing the application, I sent a copy of it to the church. They immediately complied.

The minutes clearly indicated that there was a group in council who wanted their former pastor reinstated in the church. To achieve those ends they asked the former pastor to write a letter declaring his desire to be reinstated, which he did. The former pastor's request to be reinstated deeply divided both council and congregation.

One group was of the view that the former pastor should be restored immediately and without condition. He had repented of his sins, had asked for forgiveness, and consequently there was nothing more for him to do. Although reconciliation between the former pastor and the families of the two women with whom he had inappropriate relationships was an admirable goal, his restoration should not be held hostage by the inability of certain people to forgive him. In other words, this group was of the view that restoration should come first, and if possible reconciliation.

The other group was of the view that there could

be no restoration if there was no reconciliation. The essence of the former pastor's sin was that he had taken advantage of his position as pastor. In other words, he had abused his office. A pre-requisite to being restored to that office was the reconciliation, not only of the families directly affected, but also of the whole church. It was this group's view that reconciliation had to come first and then restoration.

In order to resolve this conflict, council decided to engage the services of two ministers from the denomination. They were to recommend a procedure that could be followed to resolve this issue. On December 8, 1999, they met with council, at which time they submitted their initial report. In part the report states, "The key to be considered is the goal of the entire process. We believe the goal is not first of all the restoration of the 'former pastor' to ministry in the Christian Reformed Church."

The group in council that wanted immediate restoration was extremely displeased. Three days later, on December 11, 1999, certain members of Council held a secret elders' meeting to discuss the possibility of ousting the new pastor. This meeting created a great deal of ill-will among the members of council.

On January 5, 2000, the two denominational ministers faxed their final report to the church office. In this report they re-affirmed the position stated in their previous report, that is, that reconciliation had to come before restoration. They also had this to say about the secret meeting held on December 11:

> *We were disturbed to learn that a secret meeting such as a recent elders' meeting, which excluded your pastor was held to discuss feelings of non-confidence in your new pastor's leadership. Such meetings are very damaging to New Life, especially in its need to rebuild trust and confidence in the leadership of the church.*

The next day the president of council, who was also the leader of the group wanting immediate restoration, resigned and informed council that he would be attending another church. Thereafter, the new pastor requested a congregational meeting to deal with the differences in the congregation and to attempt to bring about some reconciliation between the two sides. The meeting was called for January 18, and was to be chaired by the new president of council who was also a member of the group that wanted immediate restoration. Without the knowledge or consent of the new pastor, the new president invited the old president of council to the meeting for purposes of explaining why he had left. Notwithstanding the objections of some, the old president spoke for about half an hour. Needless to say the meeting caused a great deal of hurt and animosity.

In an attempt to deal with the ongoing problems, council called in the church visitors. These are consultants that the church can call on for advice. They were not the same as the denominational ministers.

On January 28, the church visitors submitted their report, which stated in part: "So it also seems imperative that council be encouraged to put the reconciliation process recommended by the 'denominational ministers' in motion with a definite completion date."

On January 31, two deacons who also wanted immediate restoration of the former pastor submitted their written resignations.

In the week of March 19-26, 2000, a group from the congregation circulated a petition to assess the level of support for the new pastor. In all, 62% of the members of New Life gave their written support to the new pastor, his leadership, his ministry and his preaching. When the support of those who signed the petition was coupled with the support of those who did not sign, but who nonetheless expressed strong verbal support for the new pastor, it became abundantly clear that an overwhelming majority of the members supported the new pastor.

What the petition made clear was that in terms of supporting the leadership, ministry and preaching of the new pastor, the congregation was not divided. The division existed only in council. On March 27, another deacon from the immediate restoration group submitted her written resignation. By letter dated April 1, the new president of council (and the person who had invited the old president to speak at the congregational meeting on January 18) submitted his resignation as an elder and as a member of New Life.

On April 17, another council meeting was held. All the parties who had previously submitted their written resignations attended the meeting. Some of them had not attended a worship service at New Life for months. In fact, most of them had been attending a weekly Bible study or fellowship group with the former pastor.

At the April 17 council meeting two motions were made:

1. "That we not accept any council members' resignations until the present conflict is resolved at which time those that have submitted resignation be asked to reconsider." Carried.

2. "That Council of New Life Fellowship approach Classis with a request to approve the release of" the new pastor "from active ministerial service from New Life Fellowship because Council feels that an intolerable situation exists in the church." (Defeated by

a 5 to 3 vote).

The people who made and seconded the motion had both previously submitted their written resignations and were no longer attending at New Life. The church visitors commented on the practice of certain members of Council participating in a fellowship group with the previous pastor: "We also feel that the present participation of New Life Fellowship Leadership in a Bible study or fellowship group with the previous pastor is detrimental to the reconciliation, healing, and restoration that needs to take place."

As a result of the ongoing turmoil, and with the support of a large number of the congregation, I prepared an application to Classis Alberta North. The "Classis" is part of the governing structure of the denomination with authority over the individual churches. Specifically, the application was to compel the Council of New Life to accept the written resignations of the parties in question, and that any vacancies so created should be filled as soon as possible.

On May 24, 2000, Classis Alberta North met. At that time the following motion was unanimously carried with one member abstaining. The motion was:

MOVED that the following four points be instructions to New Life Fellowship from Classis Alberta North:

1. Insist that the letters of resignation from

council members who have submitted such letters be accepted;

2. Insist that all council members must worship regularly with New Life Fellowship;

3. Point out to Council and the congregation that Ephesians 4 makes clear that Christ has appointed leaders for the building up and the unity of his Church. Therefore, any malicious talk about the pastor or elders must stop. Any leader who has taken vows to fulfill his/her office but does not worship with the congregation is in violation of God's Word in Ephesians 4; and

4. That new council members be installed by the end of July.

Carried

I believe that the means by which a small group in council tried to have the former pastor reinstated was both untimely and wrong. It was untimely in that it was far too soon. Healing takes time and little or no effort had been made to lay the groundwork for reconciliation.

It was wrong to try to remove the new pastor to make way for the former pastor's restoration. The new pastor had done nothing wrong. Most churches would have been happy to have him. He is also a talented individual, but in a different way. He has faithfully and diligently served, and continues to serve the denomination to this day. Many people's lives have been enriched because of him.

I also think that it was especially wrong for the former pastor to try to be reinstated to the very church from which he had been deposed. The hurt he had caused to the families directly affected was deep and abiding. In addition, he knew or should have known that the letter he submitted declaring his desire to be reinstated would be divisive. I do not understand why he felt that that particular church was his only option.

In their report to the church, the denominational visitors had taken the position that the former pastor had abused his office as pastor. A pre-requisite to being restored to that office was the reconciliation not only of the families directly affected, but also of the whole church. I do not know if there has ever been reconciliation with the families directly affected. As I understand it, there has certainly never been reconciliation with the whole church. An apology would be appropriate. To quote my father, "That's a start, but you still have to make it right."

His actions, and the actions of those who supported him, led to the predictable consequences. The collateral damage was deeply felt. Families were (and continue to be) divided. Close and valued friendships were lost.

On a personal level, we very much regret the loss of the close and warm friendship of the first president of council and his wife. We have all attempted to restore something of what we had before, but to no avail.

Despite the loss, we are thankful and proud of our part in rectifying the wrong done to the new pastor. Had the small group been successful, they would have ruined the ministry and reputation of a good and innocent man.

Through this case I have a new appreciation for the governing structure of the Christian Reformed Church. In this case, Classis Alberta North was able to rectify a wrong done in a local church. This oversight is not available to what is known as "stand alone" churches. These are churches that are not part of, or affiliated with, any denomination. The parishioners in these churches are often subject to various forms of abuse and have no recourse unless they leave the church. Unfortunately, the nature of the abuse is often such that leaving is difficult.

There was such a church in Red Deer. The pastor ran the church and most of the employees were from his own family. When I was still practicing with Ben various members of his church had come to see us. In each case the complaints were similar. The complainants always came alone; usually they were the husbands, but in one case it was the wife. Their complaint was that the pastor had undue influence over their spouses. Many decisions that should have been made as a family were deferred to the pastor.

For example, the pastor always insisted that 10% of their combined income be given to the church. If the family needed a new car, a different house, or a vacation, they would require the prior approval of the pastor. In fact, they would be required to provide their income tax returns to demonstrate that the purchase would not lessen their capacity to tithe. If the income tax returns were not provided, or if the pastor doubted that the couple were properly tithing, they would be publicly called out, and placed under discipline. This meant that they could not participate in the Lord's Supper and their children would not be blessed or baptized.

Even though we encouraged the complainants to call the police or to retain us or any other lawyer to investigate the pastor, no one ever did. They said that if they did, their spouses would leave them. Although I was not retained by anyone, I was curious. On an Easter Sunday, Joyce and I decided to attend their worship service. I found the experience sickening.

After a group of gospel singers performed for approximately twenty minutes, the pastor started preaching. He preached about Christ's death and resurrection, and how we owe all to Him. His preaching style varied from loud shouts to mere whispers. He would often pause for long periods of time as he glared at the congregation.

"Even though we owe all to him," he shouted and then continued in a whisper, "there appears to be those who cannot find it in their heart to give even 10%."

"You need to know that God's coffers are empty, and no one will leave until his coffers are full," he bellowed in a crescendo of sound and motion, as he ran back and forth across the stage.

"I am going to count from twenty to one," he stated firmly, "and when I reach one, His coffers will be full," he screamed with his arms extended. "Twenty," he screamed even more loudly from mid-stage. He then marched to stage left.

"Nineteen," he shrieked, looking squarely at those in front of him. He now marched to stage right.

"Eighteen," he tried to shout again but his voice cracked. He then walked slowly to mid stage. His finger was pressed against his lips. He looked thoughtful.

"Christ gave us his all," he repeated, except that this time he appeared to be weeping, "and we can't even give him 10%," he sobbed as he wiped away the tears.

By this time I had had enough. His vocal gyrations and exaggerated gestures were driving me crazy. But it was his message that was particularly sickening. It appeared to confirm everything that we had been told. I motioned to Joyce that I was leaving. She needed no prompting.

When we approached the exit from the sanctuary, a man blocked our path.

"You can't go," he whispered.

"Why not?"

"Because he's not finished yet," he whispered again as he pointed to the pastor.

"That may be," I replied giving him my business card, "but I am. And if you don't move over, you're going to think you were born with a lawsuit." He looked at the pastor in desperation and then moved over.

I told Ben about my experience. Ben and I share a compulsion to make right what we perceive to be wrong. We talked about the various parishioners who had come to see us. We explored various options. Personally, we could not go to the police, because we had not been wronged. As lawyers we could not disclose the names of the complainants. Furthermore, we could not complain to any governing bodies. There were none and as such there was no oversight. The harm that can be inflicted by such a church cannot be overstated. Nonetheless, there was nothing we could do.

A Scoundrel And A Scam

In about 1995 Gary Zimmerman walked into my office. He was a social worker living in Red Deer. He felt burned out and for about a year he had wanted to do something different. Several months before seeing me he had been approached by an individual from Manitoba. I no longer remember the individual's name, so for now I will call him Fred Smith. Smith came to Red Deer to start a project designed to help troubled boys. The project was called "Boys Town North" and was fashioned after the well known "Boys Town" in Omaha, Nebraska.

Gary was a pleasant and interesting person. I immediately liked him. I assumed that he was in his mid forties. As he described his work I could easily imagine that he was very good at what he did. When I asked about his family he showed me some pictures. His wife was obviously attractive and he spoke glowingly of her and his children.

Somehow Smith and Zimmerman teamed up. Smith promised Gary that he (Gary) would become the first managing director of Boys Town North providing they could raise sufficient funds to get the project off the ground. From Gary's point of view the timing could not have been better. He had been looking for a meaningful alternative to social work. He was very enthusiastic about the project and his potential involvement in it.

Gary asked me if I would financially support the project and I agreed. I asked him who I should make the check out to. He said Fred Smith. I found that strange. I asked him if a trust fund or a foundation had been created for purposes of receiving the funds. He said he didn't know. Fred was collecting all the money and was working with a lawyer in town to make sure that everything was done properly. He did not know the lawyer's name. I told Gary that I was not about to write a check to someone I had never met. However I did offer to write a check payable to a lawyer's trust fund, providing he could get me the name of the lawyer.

After the meeting in our office I offered to take him for lunch. During the lunch hour I learned more about him. He was a person of deep convictions. He liked people. That was why he had gone into social work in the first place. He was one of those rare individuals who truly worked to make this world a better place. His enthusiasm for the new project could not be contained. He talked about how he looked forward to working with troubled boys. This opportunity was an answer to prayer.

He said that fundraising for the project had gone well – in fact better than expected. He did not know how much money they had already raised because Fred was taking care of the books. He himself had raised many thousands of dollars and he had also personally contributed several thousands of his own money. Fred had assured him that they would have sufficient funds to open Boys Town within a year if the contributions continued as they had.

According to Gary, Fred was a better fundraiser than he. When Fred spoke at various functions as he often did, people gave generously, especially when he spoke in churches. He said that Fred had a very powerful testimony. His testimony was that he had been a prisoner in Alcatraz, a super maximum security prison on an island off the coast of California. While in Alcatraz he had accepted God, and God had changed his life. If God could change him (one of the most hardened prisoners in Alcatraz) than surely God could change some troubled boys. In fact one elderly lady from Calgary was so enthusiastic about the project that she had given Fred her car which was almost new.

After lunch I again told Gary that I would contribute to the project providing that he provide the name of the lawyer that Fred was working with. He agreed.

Approximately a week later Gary called and said that Fred did not like his lawyer and that he was transferring the funds to a new lawyer. He would give me the name of the new lawyer as soon as he knew. He also told me that Fred was to be a participant in an ecumenical church service to be held at the Red Deer Centrium. I decided to attend.

Fred was not one of the speakers. Rather he was

the person selected to offer the prayer, but even from his limited involvement it was obvious the he was a charismatic individual and an excellent speaker.

Shortly thereafter I received a call from Fred. He began by saying that Gary recommended that he call me. After some small talk, he said that he wanted me to write a letter to the Red Deer Advocate (a daily news paper) and threaten to sue them with a libel suit. Needless to say, I asked why? He said that they were about to do a story on him and he wanted me to stop it before it was published. I asked what the story was that the Advocate was about to publish?

He explained that in his fund-raising meetings he had told his audience that he had been a prisoner in Alcatraz. While in prison he had been treated very badly. Most people would consider it torture. He often had a long, heavy chain tied around his neck, which he was required to wear continuously for weeks, even while he slept. Now the Advocate was about to publish a story that he had never been in Alcatraz and that he was a fraud.

I told him that I could not get a pre—publication ban, or even sue for libel if the story that the Advocate was about to publish was true. So I asked him, "Is it true or not?" At first he equivocated. Then he said, "Most of it is true, but it doesn't matter. If I can't say that I was in Alcatraz than I can't raise any money. People give because they believe that if God can change me then He can change troubled boys as well."

I felt that he was trying to deflect my initial question, so I pressed him. "Were you in Alcatraz – yes or no?"

"Yes," he answered, "but I was registered under a different name and I can't prove that I was there."

"What name were you using?" I asked.

"Fred Smith," he answered, "but there are no records because they were all destroyed when Alcatraz was closed in 1963."

By now I suspected that he was lying. "Do you know what libel is?" I asked.

"Yes," he answered. "It is when your reputation is destroyed."

"How does saying that you were not in Alcatraz destroy your reputation?" I questioned.

"I have a bad reputation and they will destroy it. I must be able to say that I was in Alcatraz," he repeated. "Otherwise I can't raise any money."

I told him that the law of libel probably applied only to good reputations. In any event if he could not prove that he was in Alcatraz, he had no case and I would not act for him. The real reason however, was that I did not believe him.

The next day the Advocate published the story. They said that they had investigated his claims and they had learned that he had never been in Alcatraz. In fact there was a warrant out for his arrest in Manitoba for perpetrating the same scam.

Thereafter, I never heard of Fred Smith again. He appeared to have vanished along with the money. But I did hear about Gary. I learned that he was devastated, not so much because his future was compromised, but rather because he had been a party to a fraud, albeit unknowingly. People (many of whom he knew) had been deceived. They had contributed their money under false pretenses. Gary wanted to reimburse their money, but he was unable to do so. He took no comfort from the fact that he too had been deceived, and had lost money -- probably more than most. Shortly thereafter Gary Zimmerman, the man who wanted so much to make a better life for some troubled boys, took his own life.

A Municipal Case

The third case arose out of a municipal dispute. In 1996 Joyce and I purchased a lakefront lot on Sylvan Lake, which is near Red Deer. Joyce designed the home so that almost every room had a view of the lake. An architect approved the design and drew up the blueprints. The home was built in the spring and summer of 1997 and in the fall we moved in.

It was a wonderful place to live. Sylvan Lake itself is a deep, spring-fed lake. The incoming water is almost pure. It is located in the path of a number of migratory birds and in the spring and fall of each year these birds were often seen resting on the lake.

At one time the Town of Sylvan Lake was a recreational town, alive and vibrant in the summer, but dead in the winter. Over time, however, it became the residence of choice for many people, and is now a thriving lakeside town.

In about 2001, I was elected as a councilor for the town. Most matters that came before council were routine but there was one matter that was noteworthy. It was the issue of the Sylvan Lake tree house. In February 2003, the administrative staff of the town had ordered that a tree house, built by Mrs. Armstrong's son, be removed. There were two reasons for this order:

1. There was no development permit; and

2. Even if there had been a permit, the tree house would not have complied with the town's bylaws.

My understanding was that Mrs. Armstrong lived in Calgary. When the town ordered that the tree house be removed, Mrs. Armstrong went to the press. Her complaint was that the tree house had been built for her grandchildren. They, and their little friends, had very much enjoyed it. Even though no one had complained, the town was now ordering that it be taken down because she had failed to get a development permit. What she apparently did not say was how large the tree house was or where on her property it was located.

In any event, both major newspapers in Calgary carried the story. None of the reporters had actually seen the tree house. From Calgary, the story went viral: UPI and other news gathering organizations around the world carried it. In fact, I understand that Jay Leno ridiculed the town on the Tonight Show.

Apparently, people from all over the world wrote or called Mrs. Armstrong offering support and encouragement. In contrast, the Mayor of Sylvan Lake was receiving hate mail and angry phone calls on an almost daily basis.

The matter was to come before council on August 11, 2003. Because I was quite sure that the answer would be found in the facts, I decided to investigate. What follows is a summary of the material that I prepared for council.

In the spring or early summer of 2002, construction of the tree house began. The structure measured 10 by 8.5 feet on one floor. Although it was difficult to tell from the outside, there were apparently two floors. It was erected in the front yard and according to press reports was constructed of scrap materials. The only thing "tree" about the tree house was that it was constructed around the trunk of the tree.

Furthermore, it was constructed in an area where "no accessory building or any portion thereof shall be erected or placed within the front yard" (Sylvan Lake, Bylaw No.905/86.) The town planner told me that nearly every municipality in the western world has a similar bylaw. The purpose of this bylaw is to:

1. Prohibit haphazard construction in front yards;

2. Add curb appeal to most residences;

3. Allow neighbors an unobstructed view; and

4. Allow drivers an unobstructed sightline.

Neither Mrs. Armstrong nor her son had applied for a building permit as required. The administration for the Town was not initially aware of the construction.

During the summer when the structure was approximately half-completed the Bylaw Enforcement Officer for the Town (acting on a tip) attended at the construction site. He advised both Mrs. Armstrong and her son to stop construction and obtain a development permit. Neither did as advised and the son continued with the construction.

After construction was completed, the town received a complaint from a resident of Sylvan Lake; thereafter, Mrs. Armstrong applied for a building permit. As a result of her application, the staff was required to solicit the views of the adjacent/affected landowners. The staff received six responses. Five of those who responded were strongly opposed. In addition to the written responses, some neighbors called the town. They said that they had never seen Mrs. Armstrong's grandchildren. The only person that ever used the tree house was her adult son. In fact, one neighbor told me that Mrs. Armstrong's grandchildren didn't even live in Canada. Their parents were missionaries in some foreign country and the neighbor had never seen them or the grandchildren. Another neighbor described the tree house as an eyesore. He said that it was built next to the sidewalk and he estimated the height to be about 14 feet.

Her application was denied and the structure was removed. What many people failed to understand was that the structure was unlawful, not only because of what it was but also because of where it was.

At the August 11, 2003 council meeting, the material that I had prepared was read. Copies were given to the press. As far as I know, nothing more was said or written about the infamous "Sylvan Lake Tree House."

The Painting

In the summer of 2004, shortly before I retired, I received a call from a client of mine. He gave me the following information. He was in the home of his financial adviser. He, and several others had obtained a court order permitting them to sell all the adviser's household belongings. The financial adviser had absconded with a substantial amount of their money and his whereabouts was unknown.

The reason for the call was to tell me about a beautiful mural that he thought would look good in my office. It was priced at $200. He gave me the address.

The mural was even more beautiful than he had described. It was the image of the Alberta Shield, made from real materials pressed together between glass such that the identical image could be viewed from both sides.

The cultivated wheat fields were depicted by real heads of wheat; the prairies by real grass, and the Rocky Mountains by small pieces of rock slate. The top of the shield was a flag of St. George's cross as flown by the Hudson Bay Company. The entire mural was about six feet high and three feet wide. The glass was held together with a polished oak frame. Inscribed on the base were the words "The Alberta Shield" and the name of the artist.

The Alberta Shield

It was clearly worth much more than $200. To create such a beautiful piece had obviously taken many hours. But where would I put it? It was much too large for my office. Also, how would I move such a delicately constructed mural? I seriously considered purchasing it, but eventually decided against it. It was another decision that over the years I came to regret.

While looking at the other items for sale, I found myself drawn to a particular painting. It was approximately two feet high and three feet wide. The price was $40. After about one hour I returned to the office having purchased nothing. I told Dave about the sale. He wanted to see the items as well, so together we went back. Encouraged by Dave, I offered $20 for the painting which was accepted.

The painter had signed his name as "Chardon." I knew nothing about either the painting or the painter, so that evening I googled the name "Chardon." To my absolute astonishment I learned that Chardon was a famous 18th century French painter. His paintings were nearly priceless.

Through the internet I looked at all his known paintings and compared his signature to the signature on the painting I now had. They looked identical. I then superimposed the signature on my painting over the signatures of the paintings known to be painted by Chardon. They not only looked identical, they were identical. I couldn't believe it. I had purchased a "Chardon" for $20. I immediately told Joyce of our good fortune. Together we again looked at the signatures. She agreed that they looked identical.

We discussed what to do. Should we insure it? Where could we store it? Finally we decided to try to authenticate the painting first. I opened a file and wrote the following letter to both Christie's auction house in New York and Sotheby's auction house in London.

Dear Sir/Madam
I am a solicitor in Red Deer, Alberta, and
I represent a client who purports to have a
"Chardon" painting. How can this painting be
authenticated?

Yours truly,
Winson Elgersma
B.A., B.D., LL.B

Within a few weeks both auction houses responded similarly. Both advised my client to take good quality pictures of the front and back of the painting, and send the pictures to them. If the painting appeared genuine they would send a representative to further authenticate and evaluate it.

I went home, set up some floodlights and began to take pictures, first of the front then of the back. After several photographs I noticed some wording faintly stamped on the backside of the wooden frame that I had not seen before. It took me awhile to decipher the words, but when I did, I quickly put the painting away.

I told both Joyce and my secretary what I had discovered. Both urged me to send the pictures to the two auction houses anyway. What did I have to lose? The work was done; the letters were already written and the pictures already taken. I agreed and sent the pictures.

About two weeks later I received a letter from Sotheby's. It consisted of two lines; "The painting is not a Chardon. The signature is a forgery." Christie's never did respond. I was not surprised given the words that were stamped on the backside of the painting; "Made in Mexico."

I last saw the painting in a small auction house in Red Deer. It was stacked with a number of other unsold prints and paintings. It would have been better if I had purchased the mural.

Working constantly at a high pace had taken its toll. I wanted to retire. At a certain point all new files were assigned to Dave. I wound up my existing files and Joyce and I moved to Vancouver Island. Another chapter in our life had closed.

CHAPTER 10

REFLECTIONS

Vancouver Island is a paradise. The temperatures are moderate and it rarely freezes. The winters are wet, creating a green groundcover of life. The summers are dry, enabling a variety of outdoor activities. The ocean is beautiful and the fishing is good.

Del was already practicing law on the Island; he and another lawyer had created their own firm. When we moved to the Island they already had two offices. Del wondered whether I would be interested in joining them but I was mentally exhausted and needed a rest.

I wanted to do something physical. Consequently, after we arrived on the Island, I renovated two homes including the one in which we live. However, the best opportunity for physical work came when Dave and

Laura also moved to Vancouver Island and eventually purchased a small farm. It was a beautiful property, but it needed a barn that I built for them.

The barn I built for Laura and Dave

It appears to me that my life may have taken a full circle. My first real job was to help build a barn and that may be how my working life will end. It was then that I was told that I was not indispensable. At that time I found it difficult to accept but over the years I have come to acknowledge it.

What really makes living on the Island enjoyable is

that Del and Karen (Del's wife) live nearby. We spend a considerable amount of time together. In fact, Del took the cover photo for this book while we were fishing near our home. The three orcas represent my three careers. Also when we first came to the Island Karen gave us a gift that continues to give. At one of our dinners she suggested that we recount the best of that day. Everyone including the grandchildren participated.

The practice grew and continues to the present. On birthdays, everyone says why he or she loves, or what he or she loves, about the birthday person. For the grandchildren, this means that they verbally express their love to their brothers and sisters and cousins.

On Father's and Mother's Day we do the same. Occasionally it is done in writing. The written testimonials are stored in the "important documents" file. On Thanksgiving Day everyone expresses why and for what he or she is thankful.

The grandchildren know the routine. They often think long and carefully about what to say. It makes them think positively, especially about their brothers and sisters. Their insights are sometimes surprising and often profound. Many good qualities are highlighted; various acts of kindness and consideration are tabled for all to see.

For whatever reason it is difficult for us to express our love and appreciation to those closest to us. I have often thought that the virtue of thankfulness is under-rated. It is a difficult virtue to nourish. This practice has reduced our inhibitions. Our entire family has been enriched by Karen's gift. It has taught us to express to others why we are thankful for them. It helps create a thankful heart. In fact, it was the motivation for these memoirs.

Writing these memoirs has given me the opportunity to review the whole of my life. As I became more and more aware of all I had taken for granted, I realized that I have much to be thankful for. I appreciate as never before what a precious gift life itself is. What makes it precious for myself and for others is that each life is unique. It will never happen again. It is lived but once.

I am thankful for the opportunity to live the life given me without encumbrances such as impairment or disease. I know that I may not have lived life to the fullest, but I also believe that I have not squandered it. I hope there are some, and I believe there are, whose lives are enriched because of mine.

I am thankful for the people who have been a part of my life: my parents, my brothers and sisters, my wife, my children, and my grandchildren. I realize that my children did not always have the best of everything, but they certainly made the best of everything they had.

I am thankful for the people my children have brought into my life such as my in-laws; for Karen (Del's wife) and her positive personality; for Laura Marie (Vincent's wife) whose hospitality I cherish; for Dave (Laura's husband) whose companionship I value; and for Gretchen (Chad's wife) and her indomitable spirit.

I am thankful for the family that Joyce brought into my life, including her brothers and sister and their extended families.

I am thankful for friendships and particularly life-long friendships such as Rodger and Marge Slater.

I am thankful for the people I have worked with: for Alger Braun, Ben Vanden Brink, Brad Willis and for the courageous group of ladies who helped circulate the petition in the New Life Fellowship Church. All have enriched my life.

I am thankful for lives of people that I may have been able to help or enrich: for Cathy, for Matt, for Duke, for the Beckworths, and especially for my children and grandchildren. I know that my legacy (such as it is) consists, not of what I did for myself, but rather what I did for them.

I am thankful for the opportunities in my life: for the year I spent in the bush, (it was where I grew up); for serving as a pastor in the Christian Reformed Church, (it was the most meaningful time of my life); for selling real estate, and for practicing as a trial lawyer (it was the most enjoyable time of my life).

I am thankful for both the hills and the valleys of

our lives. Someone once said that we were "three times down," referring to the three times we started with nothing. I prefer to think of it as "three times up." I may not have taken the path I planned to take, but where I ended up is where I hoped to be. Although I still don't laugh out loud, my heart is full of laughter. I have the love and respect of my intelligent and honest children, and the affections of my grandchildren. I am blessed.

I am thankful that God created me as He did: for the insight that life in the bush would be wasted, for the wisdom to marry Joyce, for the courage to leave the ministry and for the determination to carry on. I have learned that what I am is a gift from God; what I do is a gift to God.

I am thankful that God created Joyce as He did: for her steadfast Christian values, for her dedication to our family and for her loyalty to me when times were difficult.

I am thankful that my children are attempting to instill into their children the values that we (and particularly Joyce) instilled into them.

I am thankful that my children and grandchildren now include me in their lives, and occasionally ask for my advice. In the final analysis, however, I can do no better than the writer of Ecclesiastes: "Here is the conclusion of the matter; revere God and keep his commandments, for this is the whole duty of humanity."